GROUP TECHNIQUES FOR AGING ADULTS

Elders can struggle with issues of social isolation and self-esteem but benefit from having positive coping skills at their disposal. The practical ideas that Kathie Erwin imparts in this second edition help mental health professionals working with elderly populations to create an interactive, multimodal program that addresses the issues and needs that elders have. The group modalities are defined in holistic contexts of mind, body, society, and spirituality. Among the group modalities are reminiscence, bibliotherapy; remotivation; humor; expressive art; and therapeutic writing and sacred spaces, which are new to this edition. Mental health professionals appreciate the practical and detailed guidelines for how to design, implement, and monitor progress for various types of group modalities that allow them to put theory into practice easily. Their elder clients will benefit from the methods they develop in group to deal with problems such as isolation and reduced social networks.

Kathie T. Erwin, EdD, is Assistant Professor at Regent University, Virginia Beach, Virginia, in the School of Psychology and Counseling. She is the author of seven books and is a National Certified Counselor, National Certified Gerontological Counselor, a Board Certified Clinical Psychotherapist and Licensed Mental Health Counselor.

GROUP TECHNIQUES FOR AGING ADULTS

Putting Geriatric Skills Enhancement into Practice

Second Edition

Kathie T. Erwin

Routledge
Taylor & Francis Group

NEW YORK AND LONDON

First published 2013
by Routledge
711 Third Avenue, New York, NY 10017

Simultaneously published in the UK
by Routledge
27 Church Road, Hove, East Sussex BN3 2FA

Routledge is an imprint of the Taylor & Francis Group, an informa business

© 2013 Taylor & Francis

Library of Congress Cataloging in Publication Data

Erwin, Kathie T., 1950–
Group techniques for aging adults: putting geriatric skills enhancement into practice / by Kathie T. Erwin.—2nd ed.
      p. cm.
   Includes bibliographical references and index.
   ISBN 978-0-415-89783-9 (hardback: alk. paper)—
ISBN 978-0-415-89782-2 (pbk.: alk. paper)   1. Social work with older people.   2. Social group work.   3. Older people— Care.   I. Title.
HV1451.E79   2013
362.6'9—dc23   2012018560

ISBN: 978-0-415-89783-9 (hbk)
ISBN: 978-0-415-89782-2 (pbk)
ISBN: 978-0-203-08211-9 (ebk)

Typeset in Bembo
by Apex CoVantage

Printed and bound in the United States of America by Walsworth Publishing Company, Marceline, MO.

For the most fascinating group, my grandchildren:
Faith, Grace, Joseph, and Joy

CONTENTS

GROUP MODALITIES LIST

- Group Modalities for the Mind
  - Reminiscence
    - Favorite vacations
    - Lifelong learning
    - My first car
    - Childhood games
    - Birthdays
    - Seasons of the year
    - The kitchen
    - Old spices, senses, smells, and memories
    - Textiles and textures of the time
    - Family genogram
    - Decades of life
    - Life investment
  - Bibliotherapy
    - Enjoying essays
    - What's new in our city (state or nation)?
    - What's old is new again
    - Myths and fables
    - Forget TV shopping, get my catalog!
    - Attitudes about aging
    - Rhyme me a rhyme
    - Armchair exploring
    - Childhood rhymes
    - The crossroads of our lives
  - Therapeutic Writing
    - My life in three acts
    - Characters in my story

- Exploring positive feelings
- Letter to myself
- Feelings into form
- Gratitude list: Then and now
- Positive memories and early skills recognition
- Group modalities for the body
  - Body/sensory
    - Back to nature
    - Baking party
    - A bit of Florida sunshine
    - Solve the mystery without looking
    - We're forever blowing bubbles
    - The sensation of color
    - Fantastic fur and feathers—pet visits
    - Seashore sensations
    - Smooth or rough
  - Music and movement
    - Big band
    - World War II music
    - Marching
    - Patriotic
    - Nature sounds
    - Sing-Along songs
    - Trip to Hawaii
    - Outdoor concert
    - Hand bell chorus
    - Tai Chi and harp
    - Tai Chi and water music
  - Remotivation
    - Meet and greet
    - Day and month
    - Weather and season
    - Current events
    - Welcome new member
    - Beach ball toss
    - Letter-to-word association
    - Show and tell
    - Transportation
    - Rocks and shells
- Modalities for social
  - Humor
    - Classic radio comedy
    - Classic television comedy
    - Sharing jokes
    - Mature humor

- Essays
- Innocent humor of children
- Jesters of our lives
- Clowns
- Comics
- Family funnies

  o Expressive art
  - Emotions reflected in art
  - Painting
  - Paint the music
  - Soft sculpture
  - Scene drawn by group
  - Seasonal collage
  - Circles and forms
  - Sponge painting
  - Pain management
  - Message in the masters

  o Phototheraphy
  - Tell a picture story—magazines
  - Tell a picture story—family albums
  - Autobiographical photo collage
  - American life photo essays
  - A feeling collage
  - Faces of children
  - Travel by photo
  - Holiday images
  - Mature images
  - News images

- Group modalities for the spirit
  o Role
  - Birth order
  - Beliefs about families
  - Best friends
  - Work or career
  - Parenting or caregiving
  - Activities in the community
  - Clichés as imperatives
  - Rules to live by
  - The good neighbor
  - The roles of my life

  o Spirituality
  - Rituals of passage
  - Rituals of welcome
  - Life-changing moments
  - Postcards from eternity

- Spiritual companions
- Unseen comforts
- Spiritual legacy
- Spiritual symbols
- Morality and reality
- It's hard to say goodbye
- Spiritual connection to holiday traditions from around the world
- Spiritual legacy time line
○ Sacred spaces
  - Walking the labyrinth
  - Finger labyrinth
  - Meditation garden
  - Water feature
  - Shoebox altars

INTRODUCTION

The silver tsunami rolls onward as the Baby Boomer generation continues to dramatically inflate the numbers of older adults in America. Simultaneously, the cohort over age 85 shows steady growth due to increased life span. The 10–15 years after retirement at age 65 is no longer the norm, with more elders living 20–25 years after it. What does our society offer to older adults that gives them the opportunity for productivity, value, and connectedness during a longer period of old age? Purposeful, well-designed groups can be part of the solution to engaging older adults with beneficial activity suited to their age, stage, and psychosocial needs.

This book presents the original group modalities developed as Geriatric Skills Enhancement (GSE) plus a selection of new modalities. The GSE program was designed to be an interactive group program for older adults that could bridge the gap between activities or social events and psychotherapy. In collaboration with the social services staff, GSE therapists tailored the groups to address a series of psychosocial and skill concerns, most of which are common among residents of assisted care or nursing facilities as well as limited mobility elder populations in the community.

The work that was done is best expressed in the GSE Mission Statement:

> Geriatric Skills Enhancement works to restore the aging adult's sense of worth, socialization, and participation within his or her nursing home, assisted living or community organization. Each program element is planned to stimulate individuals to their highest potential level of functioning, improve mental health outlook and teach alternative coping skills.

This mission statement gives a concise explanation of the GSE approach to group work: who is served and what outcome is desired. In designing a group program for older adults, the purpose is best communicated by developing a mission statement. From that point, the details of the program can be presented to staff in a meaningful and business-appropriate manner.

Who will benefit from this book? Geriatric group leaders, gerontologists, social workers, activity directors, nursing home care planning teams, geriatric nurse practitioners, adult day care staff, and students interested in gerontology and aging issues. The modalities are presented in a format that is useful to group leaders who have varying degrees of clinical skill. The leader needs to make choices from among the modalities that are best suited to the group location, cognitive abilities, and interests of the member who will be served.

Each modality was lovingly developed and applied in a geriatric care setting. In addition to the core groups of GSE, there are new modalities. Several modalities are credited to my STAR Team (Student Associates in Research) as they completed the background research and codeveloped new approaches. The STAR Team includes Lynn Ellyn Robinson, MSCP, Troy University; Katrina Brown, CMHC graduate student, Regent University; Cynthia Burnley Trower, CMHC graduate student, Regent University; and Kelly Erwin, Human Development major at Eckerd College.

This book is organized in two sections: leader's preparation for group; and work and group modalities for the mind, body, social, and spiritual needs of older adults. Chapter 1 on Stages of Elder Groups and Chapter 2 on Designing Groups for Diverse Elder Populations establish the theoretical base for developing groups suitable to the needs of older adults at various ages and levels of functioning. Chapter 3 explains the unique characteristics necessary for an effective geriatric group leader. Chapter 4 deals with the practical issues of setting up a group in different locations, including assisted living facilities, long term care or nursing homes, adult day cares, and community centers. Chapter 5 delves into practical ideas for how to get paid for group work ranging from traditional insurance billing to alternative sources for payment.

Part 2 presents the geriatric group modalities within the four areas of mind, body, social, and spirit. These represent a holistic approach to counseling. Some of the more familiar elder group modalities appear in Chapter 6, such as Reminiscence, Bibliotherapy, and Therapeutic Writing. Chapter 7 engages the body and the senses with modalities for Remotivation, Music, Movement, and Sensory Awareness. Chapter 8 may be the most light-hearted section, in which the social needs of members are reached with modalities such as humor, phototherapy, and expressive arts. Chapter 9 touches the spiritual, not in any specific religious context, but rather the overarching issue of embracing a belief system for the end of this life and the beginning of what each elder believes is to follow. The spirit groups include exploring values and roles, spirituality, and sacred spaces. In conclusion, Chapter 10 explores the Future of Geriatric Group Work with 10 Targets for the next generation.

The best application of this book is as a launching platform for preparing a multimodal geriatric group program. Whether in a nursing home, assisted living facility, adult day care, or community center, these ideas can be mixed and used to form a core program. These modalities are also useful for students who are training in geriatric group work to practice among themselves and then apply in an elder care setting as part of a training assignment.

The objective of the author and the STAR Team is that after reading this book, you will say with confidence, "I can do that" and then proceed to create an effective geriatric group program in your community. The need for leaders competent in elder group work is growing—will you serve that need?

ACKNOWLEDGMENTS

STAR Team (**ST**udent **A**ssociates in **R**esearch): Lynn Ellyn Robinson, MSCP (Troy University); Katrina Brown (CMHC Graduate Student, Regent University); Cynthia Burnley Trower (CMHC Graduate Student, Regent University); Kelly Erwin (Human Development Student, Eckerd College). Each STAR Team member contributed research as well as designs for new modalities. From their ideas came amazing new options. Thanks for proving that you are, indeed, STARS.

Regent University, School of Psychology & Counseling—Appreciation for encouragement and support from my colleagues while working on this book.

Dr. Robert Butler, MD and Dr. Irene Burnside, RN—These gerontology pioneers are no longer with us, but they left an indelible imprint on the field and inspired me to follow their lead.

Kelly Erwin—for substantial assistance in typing and the humorous notes that accompanied each file.

Lynn Ellyn Robinson, MCSP—colleague and friend, for editing assistance and team support.

George Zimmar and Marta Moldvai of Routledge Publishing—for recognizing the value of providing this book with new group techniques for the next generation who will continue this work with older adults.

1

STAGES OF ELDER GROUPS

Therapists and leaders who are trained in group work for adolescents, young adults, middle adults, or families may have excellent backgrounds yet a totally incorrect mind-set for working with older adult groups. While many of the techniques are transferable, the overall group process, pace, and measures of effectiveness are dramatically different. The French may say "vive la différence" (long live the difference), yet for the newcomer to elder group work, these differences may initially seem odd. As the leader gains experience and witnesses the positive difference these groups can be to older adults by incorporating their long lives to make a difference for each other, this becomes worthy of celebration.

For decades, Gerald and Marianne Schneider Corey have been in the forefront of developing principles for therapeutic group process. Their classic *Groups: Process and Practice* has been the boot camp of basic group leader training for nurses, social workers, and mental health counselors from the first edition in 1977 to its eighth edition in 2010. The successive editions build on the core group progression as a four-stage model: initial, transition, working, and termination. These stages are similar in some ways to Tuckman's (1965) still popular business and coaching model for team or group development: "forming, storming, norming, and performing." In both models, the objective is to move these stages into a flow within a reasonable period of time, leading toward a planned termination date. If all works well within the group, members recognize how each other has experienced change, learning, socialization, or personal growth. These stages and outcomes play a role in geriatric groups, but with less predictability than with other adult groups. The Geriatric Skills Enhancement (GSE) program adapted existing group models for geriatric groups to these four stages: relational, transition, working, and adaptation.

Relational

In geriatric groups, more time is spent in the first stage to build rapport with new members to overcome resistance to participation in the group. Older adults, particularly those over 70, tend to be suspicious and mistrustful of anything that looks like counseling. They vividly recall the Depression, Dust Bowl, wars, and other hardships from which they were raised with a strong belief in the work ethic and self-sufficiency. The many philosophical adages like "don't cry over spilt milk" gave them a stoic approach to life problems that may now be a stumbling block that keeps them from sharing their authentic selves with the group.

The initial stage in typical groups is for introduction and ground rules, which are often done in one session. With geriatric groups, this first stage is relational because nothing beneficial will happen in the group until the leader builds relationships with members and begins to encourage them to relate to each other. For that reason, the relational stage may take two or three sessions to accomplish.

For groups within a residential long term care facility, members will be referred by staff. Residents can become suspicious of the reason they are brought to the group. When the word got out that GSE group leaders were psychotherapists and social workers, some members became anxious until one brave soul voiced the elephant-in-the-room question, "Does that mean someone thinks I'm crazy?" In the life experience of most older to oldest-old adults, elective psychotherapy was never an option. Having anything to do with psychology or counseling implied serious personal flaws and images of padded cells. Review the history of how mental patients were warehoused, abused, tormented, and disrespected as late as the early 20th century, and their fears are grounded in a wretched historical reality. It's no wonder that elders view counseling as punishment, abandonment, or spiritual compromise (Erwin, 1993). What group leaders consider commonplace about sharing feelings and gaining strength from the group dynamic, many elders see as being dragged to the principal's office and compelled under duress to answer.

Some elders will offer polite acknowledgment of other group members but keep it on a surface level. They are hesitant to form attachments within the group as a way of shielding themselves from future losses by rejecting any efforts to bond with others. At times, their feelings on this matter sound much like the disgruntled adolescent who decides to sever connections with peers rather than face abandonment or disapproval again. Elders nearing their final years of life are also wrestling with how to balance their worldviews with their present realities and resolve questions of their spirituality in an affirming rather than a guilt-laden manner.

For the group leader, the overarching goal of the relational stage is establishing trust. This requires more than explaining the purpose of the group, ways to participate, and rules for confidentiality. Older adults were also raised with the belief that "actions speak louder than words," so expect them to look to the leader as a model of trust, open communication, and positive regard. A simple, yet highly effective way for a leader to show trust is to avoid speaking in the hall or doorway to staff about group members. Even cognitively impaired older adults deserve more respect. If a discussion about a group member is needed, take it into a separate room, not a public space. Too often, insensitive staff or even physicians speak around elders as if they are not present. Such behavior is even worse when the older adult is in a wheelchair, and caregivers are literally talking over his or her head. An early incident like one of these examples is a quick way to erode trust.

Unlike Baby Boomers, the newest older adult cohorts, the older adults from their parents' and grandparents' generations have minimal experience with therapy groups or support groups. Their concept of group is family and friends or an activity-based group such as the bridge club or the bowling team. The leader must take ample time in the relational stage to create the atmosphere of friendliness and acceptance. Staying on schedule with a group plan is not as important as making the most of the initial relational stage. When done well, the stages to follow are more effective, and older adults gain a positive view of the group experience.

Transition

With cognitively aware elders, the transition stage marks a point in which group members determine whether to connect with others or remain on the sidelines. As the topics and level of discussion become less superficial, some group members blossom when given the opportunity to be heard and respected. As some blossom, others seem to fade in the background. Some older adults already have established a lifelong pattern of isolation in the crowd, a response that continues even in the small group. Some elders feel more vulnerable and lonely at this point in life and are unsure about making new connections. This dichotomy is typical at the beginning of the transition stage for elder groups.

The group leader may feel like a dance teacher attempting to persuade reluctant students to stop hugging the ballet bar and join the dance while not allowing the flamboyant students to overtake the spotlight. In other types of groups, this stage might be identified as resistance in a negative context. With geriatric groups, the leader has more to gain by promoting safe, slow steps toward participation than by challenging resistance or focusing on defenses. Although these elements may be present, a confrontational approach builds the walls higher with both the persons being challenged and those observing. As the walls go up, trust goes down. Conflicts will occur between group members and member to leader, but with geriatric groups, these conflicts tend to be more passive-aggressive.

The transition stage is a major test for the group leader who is being graded by the group on pass-fail with a minimal margin for redemption. Group members want to see how the leader handles conflict, motivates without shaming, establishes an atmosphere of trust, and models acceptance in dealing with group conflicts. Many geriatric groups spend longer in the transition stage than will other types of groups. The leader must avoid showing disappointment or pressing an agenda too rapidly. This is one of those issues in which a traditionally trained group therapist is most at risk by placing priority on a timetable. When working in a long term care facility or community agency, the leader may work with the same group for several cycles. Investing time in the relational and transition stages for the first group sets a positive tone for the following group cycle with these members.

Even experienced geriatric group leaders may find the members retreat to transition from working on occasion. The addition of new members, death of a member, changes in the physical surroundings, change of leaders, or diminishing levels of functioning of members are all factors that can impede rapid or uninterrupted movement through the transition stage.

Working

When a geriatric group enters the working stage, there is a noticeable level of cohesion, trust, and sense of personal safety. Members appropriately assume some leadership roles as they freely, without prompting, interact with others. Confrontation can occur with a positive outcome and less management by the leader than was needed in the transition stage.

A few group members are willing to attempt new behaviors, which encourages others to join. The leader may have the luxury of releasing some control and responsibility to the members in cognitively aware groups. More attention can be given to listening to the common concerns of group members and exploring how they apply what they experience in group in the environments outside of group.

In the latter years of life, elders rarely seek major changes in behavior or beliefs. The changes that emerge from the group are more often a refinement or return to expressing the authentic self. They are given freedom to be themselves, not what they think others expect an "older person" to be or do. In the working stage, group members can learn new ways to cope with physical deficits, increase self-esteem, and practice socialization in an accepting atmosphere. While fostering these skills constitutes a level of change, the focus is on practicing the skills rather than leading to a cathartic or confrontational reaction as prelude to change. The latter might work well in other types of groups, but not geriatric ones.

Corey, Corey, and Corey (2010) identify as "problem behaviors" within a group such reactions as storytelling, advice giving, silence, and dependency. These behaviors in the working stage have a different meaning for geriatric groups. An observant leader finds ways to use these behaviors positively. Storytelling is the essence of reminiscence. As long as the group leader manages situations in which storytelling by certain individuals becomes trite, repetitious, or obsessive, storytelling plays an important role in several modalities.

Advice given in "you should" or "you should not have" phrasing has no therapeutic value and needs to be redirected. However, there may be times when the
oldest-old group members can be asked to share with younger-old members how
they handle a situation, for example, dealing with lack of respect from staff in an
institutional setting. What occurs is a soft line between advice giving (judgmental,
superiority) and wisdom (how to solve a problem or manage one's own responses
to difficulty).

Silence among older adults is more often thoughtful reflection and processing
than resistance. Rather than rushing to fill the void, the leader needs to become
comfortable with silence. The silence can also be useful as a transition point to
move the group in another direction.

Dependency is not encouraged in a therapeutic context. With cognitively impaired and some oldest-old groups, however, there will be more dependency on
the group leader to guide and direct the modality even in working stage than
is the ideal for other types of groups. As in any therapeutic context, the leader
must constantly make attempts to empower the group and not use the tendency
toward dependency for his or her gratification.

In elder groups, the change in coping is accomplished by restoration of skills
that existed in younger years of the members' lives. Thus, the working geriatric
group is a reclamation group, aimed at identifying positive coping skills from the
past with reminiscence and bringing the skills, attitudes, and successes of the past
to cope with present realities. Keep in mind that not all geriatric groups reach this
level of activity in the working stage. Cognitively impaired elders may be active
within the group yet not fulfill the customary expectations of the working stage.
Here is another situation in which the leader makes the adjustment to accept and
affirm whatever degree of working is demonstrated by the cognitively impaired
group.

Cohesion in the working geriatric groups may range from high to moderate for cognitively aware elders and moderate for cognitively impaired elders.
An easy way to prompt cooperation in the working stage is to refer to being
"good neighbors." The old school concept of the good neighbor is familiar to
older adults and relates to their past experiences in helping others, friendliness,
and building relationships with persons outside the family. Keep in mind that the
older generation was also raised on the adage, "if you can't say something nice
about someone, then don't say anything." With that in mind, attempts to draw
out a quiet member by rallying the group to confront is not a suitable option.
Being openly disrespectful of a peer is not comfortable for many elders. If there
is a group member who challenges another person's behavior or responses, the
challenger may be excluded by some or all of the group members.

The intensity of the working stage can be difficult to sustain and too arduous
for the oldest-old as well as the cognitively impaired elders. When that becomes
evident, the leader needs to make adaptations of modalities or levels of intensity within a modality that can flow between transition and working stages. The

greater good is to find the level where all members are included rather than pressing to maintain expectations of the working stage.

Adaptation

In most group theories, the final stage is termination or closure. A task-specific group may have a predetermined length and end date. All members know the final meeting date and begin to anticipate or dread that final session. The leader does not wait until the final session to prepare the group for the closure. Rather, the leader builds up that final meeting as a symbolic graduation in which each member's progress is celebrated, and time is given for positive disengagement from the group. As part of the closure, the members may be asked to share what was most meaningful from the group, identify how they will use what was learned in the group, and provide suggestions that the leader may use in the next group.

Geriatric groups may be time specific, as in an intensive outpatient program, or more open ended and not time specific as part of an institutional program, community outreach, or adult day care. With open, non-time specific groups, there is no stated end date. However, there may be a change in modalities that results in a mini-closure of one modality with a group and the opening of a new modality with the same group. In a sense the group has not ended yet the focus or activity has changed.

With older adult groups, the leader can expect to manage a series of unexpected mini-closures occurring at random as the result of the death of a member, illness, or moving away from the area. These changes tend to occur with little warning. The leader must be prepared to manage these loss experiences, which supersede the current agenda and may require one or two group sessions to complete. Some long term care facilities make the mistake of ignoring the death or disappearance of a senior adult who moves away. Residents are not fooled or cajoled into ignoring a mysterious loss.

The loss of anyone who is important to the group, particularly another group member, needs to be processed at the next session. At this point, the leader switches to a grief and loss resolution focus that may also incorporate existing activities such as life review, reminiscence, or our postcards from eternity. Allowing the older adults to use the group as a safe place to grieve and talk about how this loss affects feelings of their own mortality is a way that the leader demonstrates respect and genuine regard for each member. Wrapping up this mini-closure time with verbal tributes about the missing member can be some of the most cohesive and profound moments that the group will share. In grief, their guard is down and their emotions can surface. From these closure points, the leader shows honor for the departed member and by that openness, which may not be present from staff, the leader further earns trust. From this closure, members begin the adaptation of becoming a smaller group or bringing a new member into the group.

Dealing with the adaptation stage differs slightly for community dwelling elders. From living within the larger community, they have more contact with people of various ages than do those who live in long term care facilities. The young-old (60–70) living in the community may still drive, live independently, and are less adversely impacted by age-related physical conditions (Toseland & Rizzo, 2004). Community dwelling elders in a community program are generally more mobile whether they drive or use other transportation. Because of their sustaining connection to their community, these elders are more likely to bring external issues into the group discussion such as changes in Medicare, scams preying on the elderly, or the price of groceries. This gives the leader an additional source of material to use in discussions by choosing current events within the immediate area where members live.

Community dwelling elders may be more vocal because they are only in group for a short time and return to their homes later. The aspect of distance between living space and group location allows community dwelling elders to be controversial or opinionated without concern for offending those on whom they depend, as is the case with elders in long term care.

The leader cannot let the appearance of independence shown by some community dwelling elders obscure that they deal with the same loss of roles, family, friends, health, and connections that are faced by those who live in long term care facilities. Aging and cohort effects are the great levelers in geriatric group work.

2

DESIGNING GROUPS FOR
DIVERSE ELDER POPULATIONS

The first step in group design is to reject the ageist assumption that older adult groups are simple to design. There is no one-size-fits-all geriatric group modality. Some modalities may cross cohorts, working well with the young-old as well as the old-old, but only to the extent that group tasks have been adapted for each group. Geriatric groups are as much art as science. Perhaps surprisingly, it was the words of an 18th-century poet, not a social scientist, who captured the essence of what older adults need in group work:

> One ought, every day at least, to hear a little song, read a good poem, see a fine picture and, if it were possible, to speak a few reasonable words.
>
> Johann Wolfgang von Goethe

From the poetic to the practical, Goethe's recommendation served as the foundation for the elder groups that combined music, reading, fine arts, and discussion. What older adults often lack in their daily schedule is a variety of engaging activities that stimulate differing social, verbal, and physical skills. These groups provide a structured process for older adults, who may have outlived close friends or family members, to begin new connections and discover the group as a new opportunity for socialization and possibly for some new friendships (Park, 2009; Rook, 2009; Street & Burge, 2012). Whether living in the community or assisted care, Shaw, Krause, Liang, & Bennett (2007) found that there is a "dynamic nature of social relationships in late life" that underscores the value of providing interactive, purposeful groups.

From the therapeutic side, geriatric group therapy is multimodal in the tradition of Arnold Lazarus. The geriatric group therapist is continually alert to the elements of Lazarus's BASIC ID: behavior, affect, sensation, imagery, cognition, interpersonal relationships and drugs (Lazarus, 1976). While not a new concept, the BASIC ID remains valuable in evaluating the needs of each elder group and for monitoring those needs within the group. The GSE group approach goes one step beyond to BASIC IDS, adding an "S" for attention to the spiritual dimension. This is not a specific denomination or belief system but rather acknowledging and working with the spirituality of each elder. As elders reach Erikson's (1950) final stage of Integrity v. Despair, spirituality can become a source of strength in resolving important unanswered questions and making satisfying connections necessary to finish well.

Toseland and Rivas (2005) divided group modalities into those focused on treatment as different from task. In their context, treatment groups were ongoing and leading toward a therapeutic goal that differs from a task group that may be for a specific time period or a special stated purpose (Toseland & Rivas, 2005). In the GSE approach, geriatric groups can be a blend of both purposes: therapeutic and task built around a specific goal (McCarthy & Hart, 2011). For geriatric groups, the therapeutic goals may be broader and more inclusive than in other adult therapy groups such as addictions ones. Task specific groups in geriatric context are also targeted modalities like reminiscence, music, or remotivation.

Initial Planning Decisions

Whether the planning for geriatric groups is done by a group therapist or a facility treatment team, there are 10 basic questions to be considered in group design:

1. What is the age range of the group member population?
2. What is the physical layout of the group space?
3. How mobile are the group members? Is additional staff required to safely transport members to the group?
4. Will this group be one module within an existing program or a stand-alone group?
5. Are group members of comparable mental status? Combining cognitively intact and cognitively impaired individuals in the same group is complicated and of questionable therapeutic value.
6. What ethnicities are represented within the group membership?
7. What adjustments can be made so that members with physical impairments can fully participate?
8. Does the group activity require writing, reading, movement, or hearing?
9. What are the overall treatment goals for this group? How will progress for each member be documented?
10. What level of skills and experience are required for the group leader?

The answers to these questions are critical to help the group leader select appropriate modalities to meet the therapeutic objectives for each group.

Planning Groups for Cognitively Impaired Elders

GSE's cognitively impaired elders reside in dementia care units within a long term care facility. In some cities, there is an increase in the number of adult day care programs that offer dementia care for elders who are ambulatory and in early stages of dementia. Based on what is learned in the assessment process and discussion with staff, the group therapist can determine which combination of elders is suitable for a given group. Care facilities in which the cognitively impaired elders are included in groups with cognitively aware elders may work to a limited degree in small settings but run the risk of diminishing social interactions for both populations (Park et al., 2012; Burge & Street, 2010). This is further support for the GSE concept to maintain separate groups so that each obtains maximum benefit from the program and supports in-group socialization. The ultimate test of accurate group placement occurs in the initial stages of group activity. Be prepared to make changes as needed in group composition if the mix is volatile or disagreeable for reasons that may be impossible to anticipate.

Many of the themes presented in this book are suitable for cognitively impaired elders with some adaptation. The critical factor in making plans for this group is to coordinate modalities with a particular group's overall level of functioning and expressed interests. Be mindful that these are group members who have dementia, not dementia patients in a group. This distinction speaks volumes about the therapist's sensitivity. Considering the behavioral and memory challenges, choose modalities that minimize cognitive deficits and enhance present skill levels of the group members (Lindeman, Downing, Corby, & Sanborn, 1991). Begin to access group participation abilities with one remotivation group weekly and rotate other themes.

Regardless of modality, establish a routine group opener in which the group therapist greets each member individually and encourages him or her to greet the group. As a simple remotivation exercise, the opener may include a brief reality orientation exercise such as something unique about the month (October: falling leaves, wearing sweaters). Efforts to drill the exact date and time are frustrating and represent an old attitude of forcing a memory-impaired person to remember information that is confusing. This is a guaranteed way to ruin the start of a group.

Always have one or two activities that are enjoyed by the group. This is the backup plan for days when group members are notably edgy or when there are other distractions in the facility such as repair workers in the hallway or the sudden arrival of emergency medical services. The backup plan is also valuable for days when the group loses interest in the planned modality. At least make every effort to finish the session on a positive note.

One observation from lower functioning memory-impaired groups is the tendency to lose interest in the primary modality midway into group. Here's where knowing the group cohort history makes all the difference. Something as simple as starting a sing-along of old favorite songs from the 1930s or 1940s for a few minutes can be sufficient change of pace to revive interest and return to the planned modality. The group leader has to be creative and flexible enough to respond to the group's unspoken messages of boredom, frustration, and restlessness.

Planning Groups for Adult Day Care and Community Elders

Whether living independently or with family, community dwelling elders have psychosocial needs similar to those of cognitively aware elders in residential care. In these groups, leaders work without the advantage of social history, diagnostic background, and staff observational information to supplement the initial assessment. Adult day care programs have basic intakes and the potential to meet family members who could provide more useful information about the older adult's social and occupational background. With community dwelling elders, such as those attending a local senior center or church-based program, the leader will have to depend on group intake information provided by the prospective group member.

Adult day care populations may be more stratified by cognitive functioning than are community programs. A group therapist or leader may be contracted to provide specific types of groups for these older adults based on space availability and overall needs of the participants that are not met with existing activity programs. Groups focused on reminiscence, bibliotherapy, music, and movement blend well into the adult day care schedule with minimal additional requirements. After establishing groups and demonstrating professionalism to the staff, the leader has earned the opportunity to propose additional modalities to expand the program.

Providing group work for community dwelling elders meets needs of a largely ignored population. Older adults who are capable of independent living still have socialization needs that are not well met for those who are isolated by choice or mobility limitation (whether physical or lack of transportation). While community dwelling elders may have mobility and even adequate financial resources, they can begin to withdraw if they lose significant social connections and are not able to find substitutions for formerly satisfying social networks (Rook, 2009). These older adults are at risk for depression, which is a common factor in suicides among persons over age 65—even those who have had recent medical care (Conwell, 2001). Fostering cohesion within the group is an overarching goal that increases a sense of belonging and acceptance within the group that may not be present in casual social connections (Yalom & Leszcz, 2005). In addition to the issues of aging, community dwelling elders are constantly subject to age discrimination and social barriers. Ageism is an equal opportunity offender, in which age is a greater barrier than ethnicity to full social and economic participation in the community. Fueled by stereotypes, both negative (such as old people are slow and senile) or positive (the cheerful cookie-baking granny), these social role assignments can alter an older adult's functional independence and cognitive abilities (Bennett & Gaines, 2010). Whatever affects their emotional state, such as dealing with ageism in a particular situation, can become a potential group discussion. Leaders who remain aware of these issues can effectively integrate them into a modality to allow processing, support, and possible problem solving. This group may be the only forum in which an elder feels comfortable sharing personal concerns or expressing opinions without criticism.

Community dwelling elders are typically self-directed and have chosen to "age in place," that is, to remain in their prior home or city rather than move nearer adult children or into a retirement village in the Sun Belt states. For them, a group program must be attractive, accessible, and authentic. Piquing their curiosity about the themes and emphasizing the socialization makes the group seem more attractive. An accessible location for groups needs to be easy to find, have nearby parking, wheelchair accessibility, and be preferably downstairs or with a reliable elevator. To be authentic, groups must provide a realistic opportunity for all participants to learn, interact, and enhance their well-being. As Street and Burge (2012) wisely note, it is difficult to measure "well-being" that is largely self-reported. However, their concept of "adaptive reframing" in assisted living can also be applied to community dwelling elders who have other influences, both positive and negative, that impact their sense of well-being and are, by living in the community, less limited by the group experience than those in assisted living.

Another characteristic of community dwelling elders is that they retain strong connections to their family, friends, neighbors, and cultural heritage. The group leader needs to know as much as possible about the cultural identity of all group members, particularly those from ethnic minorities. Never assume that an older adult who has lived in the same city for most of his or her life has fully assimilated into the dominant culture. Strong familial ties and a love of the birth heritage continue throughout life, regardless of the country of origin and present citizenship. Appreciating this diversity within groups is important for all members to feel valued and willing to share with others.

Diversity and Elder Group Planning

Begin with what Ivey, Pedersen, and Ivey (2001) call "multicultural intentionality," in which the group leader is proactively incorporating the ethnicities and cultures represented in a given group. The diversity within the elder group is likely a reflection of the local or area population as well as the changing cultural composition of the nation. Among older adults as well as younger cohorts, the Hispanic population is expected to have the most dramatic growth. Hispanic elders will increase from 7% in 2010 to 20% of the population by 2050 (U.S. Census Bureau, 2010). The racial distribution among adults over age 65 in 2050 is projected to be 77% White, 20% Hispanic, 12% Black, 9% Asian, and the reminder divided among smaller racial groups of American Indians, Alaskan Indians, Hawaiians, and other Pacific Islanders (U.S. Census Bureau, 2010). Keep in mind that these are national population patterns and may not reflect the diversity within a given community.

The group leader needs to be knowledgeable about the racial and ethnic minorities in the community and those who will be part of the group program. Just as the oldest-old (over 80), White Americans shared a Depression era spirit to survive adversity and a general cultural taboo to "not air your dirty laundry in public," other cultures also have a distrust of therapy or sharing personal feelings with strangers. Whether the group leader is male or female may be received differently according to ethnic views. Even something as basic as making eye contact between the leader and a participant might be received negatively by an elder even though the leader was only doing what seemed, in his or her cultural context, to be the way to engage interest. A group leader who is not well versed in the traditions and communication styles of minority members needs to learn more in order to properly incorporate minority members into the group. To invite (never insist) the minority members to teach the group about their traditions is a gentle way to motivate participation and to give honor to the cultures represented in the group. Look for ways to bring cultural context into the group modalities.

The group leader needs to understand and accept the cultural differences between him- or herself and the minority group members. For example, typical American thinking emphasizes mastery over self and environment, while American Indians and Asian Americans are satisfied to be in harmony with others and nature. Be aware that some older adults have had minimal contact with minorities and may still hold negative stereotypes from bygone days. African American elders recall life under segregation where there was a broad distrust of Whites in authority, which may carry over initially to feelings on a White group leader. Extended family and internal family hierarchy are so strong with Hispanics and Asian Americans that their older adults may seem reluctant to talk about feelings or self with persons outside the family (Sue & Sue, 1990).

For these minorities as well as all elders, the leader earns the leadership role by showing respect and genuine acceptance without regard to ethnic origin. Begin by addressing all group members as Mr., Mrs., or Ms (some may prefer to be Miss) unless they grant permission to use first names.

This sign of respect is particularly important when working with community dwelling elders or those in adult day care. Older adults in residential facilities are more accustomed to being addressed by first names. Whatever the protocol is in the residential facility, do the same since residents are familiar with that approach.

A review of ideas for working with diversity in group can be found by studying the Association for Specialists in Group Work's 1999 "Principles for Diversity Competent Group Workers" and the multicultural competencies recommended by Sue and Sue (2003). Group leaders are advised to learn as much as possible about the multicultural heritage of group members before the first group.

Additional information about particular aspects of culture can be gleaned from studying, talking with other therapists experienced in working with those cultural groups, and from sincere conversation with the minority elders.

Designing Groups for Baby Boomer Elders

The U.S. Census analysis of the "Next Four Decades: 2010–2050" (May 2010) indicates that the major change in elder population will be due to the aging of the Baby Boomer generation and immigration. The full Baby Boomer population (born 1946–1964) will pass age 65 by 2030, which will swell the rank of older adults from 13% in 2010 to 19% by 2030 (U.S. Census Bureau, 2010). The Baby Boomers continue to break barriers as they did in the wild '60 by pushing the culture to adapt to them and now by kicking aside the current concept of aging.

A study by the Center for Health Workforce Studies (2006) found that the new elders entering from the Baby Boomer generation have more racial and ethnic diversity with a larger population of Hispanics and Asians than in prior older cohorts. The aging Boomers have more education; wider access to information (largely online); and greater awareness of social resources, all of which are predictors of higher usage of health services (p. 2). Another positive factor is that Baby Boomers cut their teeth on groups as young adults from transactional analysis to Gestalt to drug treatment groups, so the concept of group therapy will be neither novel nor intimidating as it is to older adult cohorts. For the group leader, this means less resistance to the format and potentially starting with participants who have experience with group therapy.

Designing Groups for Caregivers and Families

With community dwelling elders, the family and the caregiver (who is typically a family member or spouse) who are also older adults can benefit from geriatric groups. A community center or faith-based organization can easily integrate some of the geriatric group modalities into their senior adult programs. By setting aside a group for caregivers, these group members have the opportunity to talk with others in the same situation while working together on the group modality. This is a double advantage for caregivers and caregiving family members who are struggling with the demands of caregiving as they also face their own issues of aging.

The group does not have to revolve around caregiving, in fact, better that it does not become mired in care details. Caregivers need an emotional lift from their responsibilities and a time to socialize—which the group can provide. Choosing some of the lighter topic modalities such as from humor, art, or music is a good place to start building rapport among the group. Some aspects of reminiscence or spirituality may become intense particularly as the death of the care receiver is near or has recently occurred. The group leader needs to treat this situation with respect and compassion without turning the session into a bereavement group. Keep in mind that bereavement groups are complicated processes that need to be facilitated by trained professionals, not volunteers or students. If there are sufficient individuals interested, the community center or faith-based organization can bring in a psychotherapist or social worker with bereavement group experience to lead that group. Otherwise, the coordinator needs to have ready information on bereavement groups with Hospice or another appropriate local program.

Typically, caregiver groups affiliated with hospitals, assisted living, or long term care centers are focused on caregiving issues. These institutions would be wise to consider offering alternating sessions or separate groups for caregivers that focus on their needs, their creativity, and their enjoyment as a valuable "therapy" for these dedicated individuals.

Turning a Smorgasbord into a Multicourse Feast

The modalities presented are from the original GSE group design refined over several years with new additions to expand the options. Rather than being like a smorgasbord with too much piled on the plate to focus on the experience, start with appetizers or basic group modalities that serve as introductions to the program and fit well with most settings. From that point, build the program by choosing the modalities that best serve a given elder population. When prepared with purpose and properly served, each modality satisfies a particular hunger and prepares the emotional palate for another stimulating experience. Over time, each leader adds style and creativity to the groups as a fine chef does in preparing a gourmet feast. Bon appétit!

3

GROUP LEADERSHIP

Are You Right for This Work?

Group work with elders requires more direction, encouragement, empathy, psychological support, and leader interaction than with other adult groups (Burnside, 1973). While that may seem like a tall order, keep in mind that a degree in gerontology is not a guarantee of success as a geriatric group leader. Other characteristics and abilities are a greater predictor of success and satisfaction in working with aging adults. The most effective geriatric group leaders possess these essential qualities:

- Genuine interest in working with older adults
- Belief that elders have a right to pleasure, socialization, personal growth, and unconditional respect regardless of age, physical limitations, or cognitive impairment
- Enjoyment in being creative and flexible in leading groups
- Willingness to seek continuing education and training to further skills in geriatric group work and therapeutic issues of aging
- Excitement about the potential for program development that contributes to the body of knowledge about group work for aging adults

Attitudes about Aging

Whether a prospective group leader is in the demographic category of graduate student, middle-age adult, or young-old adult, each leader comes to this work with sociocultural attitudes about aging. This is different than diagnostic groups where the psychotherapist or nurse has the professional training to lead a group but will never experience exactly what the group experiences. It is possible to be an effective leader for a group of persons with schizophrenia or depression without knowing firsthand what it is like to have those conditions. Aging is different. Regardless of the leader's age, he or she will grow old and acquire firsthand experience. Working with older adults is to see one's future.

The geriatric group leader who relates best with older adults is a person who can see himself or herself in the group members. These are not merely "old people with problems." These are individuals with vast life experience, fascinating stories, and who had a front row seat to significant historical events that have shaped our modern world. The man struggling down the hallway on a walker was a record holding long-distance runner in high school and an alternate for the Olympic team. The woman clutching a blanket may have less short-term memory today, but the feel of that material takes her back to the 12 children she raised: hers and those she took into her home after her sister's death. Imagine yourself in this situation because if you live long enough, you will be. Would you want to be known for present limitations or for the essence of who you have been over a lifetime? Williams and Warren (2009) caution all staff working with older adults to avoid labeling a behavior as personality. When any staff member or group leader begins to characterize an older adult as rude or disruptive, that assumption sets up a negative expectation that becomes an ongoing communication problem.

Marianne Corey suggests that in preparing for group work with older adults the leader needs to ask himself or herself the tough questions like "how would you like to be viewed . . . attended to?" (Corey, Corey, & Corey, 2010). Another aspect of self-evaluation is to consider how the leader would want someone to treat his or her parent or grandparent in a similar setting?

Take it back to the old saying of "walk a mile in my shoes," and contemplate whether as a group leader you have the ability to respect and empathize with older adults. If leading a geriatric group is a job assignment or what the newest students are stuck doing because the other groups are taken, then you are not right for this work and have the potential to be damaging to others.

Geriatric groups are one of the new frontiers for serving the needs of a growing elder population. Some colleagues have teased me about how geriatric therapy was a yawn—working in slow motion along with the elders. What they fail to understand is that the tempo of geriatric group work places considerable demands on the leader's energy, attentiveness, and resourcefulness. After the third GSE group on any day, my feeling was more of perpetual motion than slow motion. Geriatric group work is not for leaders who like to quickly reach the working stage, then sit back and let the members do most of the challenging and accountability among themselves. With geriatric groups, the leader can expect to be the spoke of the wheel from which activity begins and through which most action passes. Here's the secret about geriatric group work: Older adults are gracious, respectful, and appreciative of the group leader. As a result, geriatric group leaders can expect to be drained at the end of group yet enjoy the satisfaction of making a difference among an often neglected population.

Developmental Issues

Regardless of degree, professional training, or experience, the geriatric group leader needs to understand the developmental stages of later life. Aging adult group members are part of Erikson's (1950) final stage of psychosocial development, Integrity v. Despair. In this final life stage, adults over age 65 reflect on their lives and decide whether they feel fulfillment or despair at what has or has not been accomplished. Older adults who can look at the successes and failures in their lives with a feeling of overall satisfaction are more likely to cope with aging issues. Those who dwell on the "half full glass" or allowing the failures in life to obliterate any successes reach older age with bitterness and less resilience for illness, mobility limitations, and other losses of aging. Understanding the dichotomy in this final Eriksonian stage helps to make sense of why older adults do not fit the myth that age automatically results in wisdom, patience, and kindness.

While Erikson's psychosocial theory applies to any adult over age 65, there are actually four distinct cohorts among older adults: middle-aged old (55–64), young-old (65–74), old (75–84), and oldest-old (85+) (Seccombe & Ishii-Kuntz, 1991). In examining which groups might be more pessimistic as a result of their present age, Seccombe and Ishii-Kuntz (1991) started with the assumption that those at both ends of the aging cohort would be more pessimistic. What they found was that the middle-old were more pessimistic about their current life stage whereas the oldest-old had come to terms in an optimistic manner. Geriatric group leaders need to be aware of the distinctions between these age cohorts. For example, with music, the oldest-old will delight to big band tunes while the middle-aged old come from the rock and roll background. The oldest-old usually remember in detail where they were the news came over the radio about the bombing of Pearl Harbor while the middle-aged old and some of the young-old were not born when that historical event rocked the world.

Coping with Losses

With older ages comes the need to cope with problems that some adults never experienced before—such as using a walker or wheelchair, giving up driving a car, distress of chronic pain, and fear of outliving financial resources. Imagine being the last of your siblings or friends to survive as your spouse, relatives, friends, and even adult children die. These compounded grief and loss experiences leave many older adults dependent on staff or home care workers. Geriatric group leaders need to identify the coping abilities and coping styles of group members. With the physical deficits and emotional stresses, the old and oldest-old become focused on managing within their living space or community and holding onto as much autonomy as possible (Ryff, Kwan, & Singer, 2001). When the group is composed of nursing home or assisted living residents, the nursing staff may be able to provide information on how they have seen these older adults cope with losses. Keep in mind that empathy is not properly expressed by what Williams (2006) called "infantilization of residents" where older adults are spoken to as if they are children or less able to understand. A former nursing home resident revealed to *AARP The Magazine* the frustrations caused by being addressed as hollow sounding "endearments . . . idiotic we's . . .hi hon . . . [and] chirpy singsong voices" (Corbett, 2007). Even when dealing with persons who have dementia, this is a poor communication style.

With community dwelling elders, there is often less advance information so the group leader discovers the coping style of members as they discuss reactions to current or past events. Exploring themes in reminiscence or life review modalities are useful ways to draw out information about coping styles among the members.

Overcoming Stereotypes

The social and cultural stereotypes of aging intrude into every geriatric group. America glorifies youth, vigor, and independence. With advanced age, these are compromised then lost forever with ravages of illness, mobility limitations, cognitive impairment, and changes in physical appearance. A few wrinkles and gray hairs signal the beginning age-related physical changes that lead to devaluation in an ageist society.

Regardless of the level of education or professional status, whether volunteer or student, group leaders have to acknowledge the stereotypes about aging that they have. Toseland and Rizzo (2004) caution that elder group workers are initially influenced by their "vicarious experiences with grandparents and other elders." There are many negative stereotypes about aging adults as incompetent, grumpy, or useless, which are reinforced in jokes, movies, and behavior toward older adults whose slower reactions inconvenience younger adults in the grocery line.

Graduate students and some volunteers in their 20s and 30s may feel peculiar about being "in charge" of a group that is the age of their grandparents or great-grandparents. They may hesitate to fully embrace the leadership role because of the age differences. Other young adults who had contentious relationships with older adult relatives can go the opposite direction and be overly controlling. What was intriguing to learn in developing these aging groups, as a middle-age adult therapist, was that many of our group members considered me to be a young adult. Needless to say, there are always a few older adults who will challenge "youthful" leadership, whether the leader is 21 or 41. When a group leader is effective in showing the Rogerian concept of "warm positive regard" in the relational stage, the issue of age diminishes rapidly.

Developing Group Bonds

While the leader's role is more directive in geriatric groups, never underestimate the therapeutic benefit of the group members toward each other. Yalom's

(1995) classic approach to group work was based on his belief that the acceptance, interaction, and support of group members could be as significant as anything the group leader provides. In geriatric group work with community elders and cognitively aware residents in nursing homes or assisted living, the potential positive impact of these characteristics within the group are amazing to witness. At this point, the wise group leader steps back to encourage the group members as they support each other. The findings of Street, Burge, Quandagno, and Barrett (2007) that residents are more satisfied when they develop positive bonds with staff members can reasonably be applied to group members who show more interest in and participation with the group when they have a positive bond with the group leader.

The most memorable example of a strong group bond with the leader and each other occurred in a GSE group with members ranging in age from 67 to 95. Therapeutically speaking, the commonality among this varied age group were their diagnoses of depression and adjustment disorder since entering long term care. To keep the facility staff from saying "Depression Group," we euphemistically referred to them as the "D" group. When asked, we said that they were the fourth group in our program, which they took to be an alphabetical title. What we did not know is that the "D" would transform to delight.

The mixed ages proved to be a struggle in several modalities, much the way it might be to expect a high school student to enjoy the same activities as a first grader. In an effort to create unity, we asked them to consider this group as a family with different ages yet common interests. In a magical moment, the 95-year-old male and 94-year-old female agreed that they could be the parents for the struggling, lonely 67-year-old woman who felt too young to be in a nursing home. The old and young-old members also chose roles: three wanted to be aunts while the other two decided to be a big brother and a big sister. For several months that the group remained together, we took time during each session to play out those roles. Even more significant was the report from staff that these group members showed their "family" roles when we were not together in group. These eight people demonstrated that the value of connection transcended many obstacles of aging, illness, and the eventual death of the "parents." We marveled at what was truly a mountain top experience for any geriatric group leader. What began as a way to create belonging among the group became empowerment when they connected as a family of choice. After sparking the idea, the best thing we did was stay out of the way to observe what happened as the best of geriatric group therapy unfolded before us. Effective group leaders know when to stop leading and go with the flow.

Before defining professional and volunteer roles, be aware that in this book there is a determined effort to show opportunities for willing leaders from various levels of training. To avoid any semblance of professional hierarchy, the term "group leader" is used to refer to individuals from both professional and lay backgrounds. Some group modalities are psychotherapeutic in nature and need to be led by psychotherapists, nurses, or psychologists. This is not to be exclusive, merely mindful of the best interest of the older adult group members. A substantial number of the group modalities in this book can be adapted for leadership in a variety of settings by professionals, students, or volunteers.

Nurse as Group Leader

Nursing programs provide exceptional training for group leadership because of the education in gerontology and aging issues. Nurses were pioneers in developing geriatric group work within both geropsychiatry programs and nursing homes. An early article (Yalom & Terrazas, 1968) published in the *American Journal of Nursing* on geriatric group work in a hospital setting was coauthored by a nurse (Terrazas) and a renowned expert on group work (Yalom). Two seminal books that set the standard for geriatric group work are by nurse-author Irene Burnside: *Psychosocial Nursing Care of the Aged* (1973) and *Working with Older Adults: Group Process and Techniques* (Burnside & Schmidt, 1978). Nurse educators Dr. Burnside and Dr. Schmidt produced three editions of this work but did not live long enough to complete the next edition. Keeping alive the nurse-scholar tradition learned from these pioneers, the fourth edition of *Burnside's Working with Older Adults* (2005) was finished by nurse colleagues Dr. Barbara Haight and Faith Gibson. Considering the long tradition of geriatric group work by nurses, nursing journals are an excellent source of practical ideas for implementing a geriatric group program.

As a response to concerns of disorientation, lethargy, and isolation of senior adults in both hospitals and nursing homes, nurses led the way in defining approaches for reality orientation and remotivation groups. Another modality that is often referred to as the "nurses' group" is an important way for teaching patients and caregivers about proper medication use, nutrition, sensory stimulation, and personal care within the limits of specific illness or physical disability. These group experiences are solid background for expanding into geriatric group modalities. Nurses who have advanced training in behavioral interventions, psychosocial deficits, and cognitive impairment are prepared to lead more intense psychotherapeutic elder groups with minimal additional training. Other nurses who have worked in nursing homes, assisted care, or community nursing with elder patients can easily adapt their skills to group work.

Therapist/Social Worker as Group Leader

Social workers, both Licensed Clinical Social Workers and those with undergraduate degrees, are often in charge of therapeutic work within long term care facilities. Their work differs from activity directors or social directors when the group focus is therapeutic in design with specific goals and outcome measures that address the needs of each group member.

Psychotherapists, Licensed Professional Counselors and Licensed Mental Health Counselors may be brought into a facility or community program for group work or other individual counseling. Clinical Psychologists may supervise therapeutic programs, consult on specific cases, or conduct assessments for the treatment team and are less likely to be group leaders.

Regardless of degree, the bare minimum qualification for group leadership among potential graduate and undergraduate group leaders is a solid foundation in group facilitation and experience or supervision in leading adult groups of various ages. Interest is growing in geropsychology as psychologists and psychology interns are moving beyond nursing home services and into services for assisted living residents (Karel, Gatz, & Smyer, 2012). Training in gerontology and geriatric groups is a plus, yet much of this training for therapists is obtained by post-degree continuing education. A minority of baccalaureate and graduate schools in psychology and counseling include aging or gerontology within the core curriculum. The most that these students know about gerontology is what they glean from some of the developmental theories and possible mention of the burdens on a marriage and family due to caregiving for aging adults. Aging studies and gerontology are, at best, an elective even though the dramatic population changes among the growing older adult population will impact therapists in many types of professional practice.

As previously mentioned, the effective geriatric group leader must temper expectations of progress learned in traditional group therapy with younger adults in order to set a reasonable pace for the older adult groups. Therapists and social workers who have worked with young children already know how to be patient and attuned to nonverbal cues such as those that are seen among older adults who are socially isolated or cognitively impaired. Other useful experience includes group leadership with individuals who have emotional or physical disabilities. Therapists and social workers who are accustomed to working with clients who have challenges with digital dexterity, mobility limitations, or visual deficits will recognize the need to adapt group activities to those older adults who are differently abled or need further assistance.

Volunteer/Student as Group Facilitator

Community groups such as congregate dining, faith-based elder groups, retirement residences, or senior centers are less likely to have licensed professional therapists or nurses among the regular staff. These sites may be directed by a social worker or an agency worker as well as dedicated volunteers. In these settings where the participants are cognitively aware older adults, the groups tend to be activity and entertainment oriented. However, there are many GSE modalities that could be used in this setting with volunteers who are willing to obtain additional training and/or supervision from an experienced geriatric group leader.

University students in psychology, counseling, nursing, or gerontology are also ideal candidates to serve as volunteer group leaders in community settings. These programs present opportunities for internship under the university guidelines, which gives the community program access to additional group leaders as well as professional guidance from the university supervisor.

Volunteer leaders must avoid the same problem as lay leaders in support groups, that is, taking on the leadership role for the wrong reasons. Group leadership is not the place to work out the leader's issues, attempt to force changes among the members' belief systems, or treat the session like a social event. With group leadership, there is a responsibility to put the needs of the members ahead of any personal agenda the leader has. Volunteers as well as professionals must be willing to expand their concept of what it means to age and the needs of each aging cohort.

Returning to sage advice from Burnside and Schmidt (1994), volunteers need more than a casual orientation and an identified supervisor. Within a long term care facility, the supervisor can be a nurse or activity director who will observe the volunteer in group and show him or her how to make corrections as needed. The process is not as formal as that of clinical supervision for counseling or doctoral students as group leaders. However, there is a tendency in some over-worked long term care facilities or volunteer–run community programs to eagerly turn the program over to a willing volunteer without any supervision.

Another role for volunteers and students is as coleaders with a therapist or nurse. Community groups can be larger than the groups selected for work within a long term care facility so the additional person to assist is valuable. Volunteers with certain skills such as music, painting, photography, or drama are welcome additions to bring their unique talents to any community or long term care group. Consider inviting retired older adults to volunteer. Retired volunteers who are mobile and active bring a new dimension to working with their peers as well as the secondary benefit that volunteering gives to their emotional well-being (Pilkington, Windsor, & Crisp, 2012). That's a win–win situation.

The fear that a group might become challenging or react negatively to a modality is largely managed by the choice of modalities. With volunteer or student leadership, the modality options need to be those that are less inclined to bring up negative emotions from past situations. While there are no guarantees in how members may react, there must be a person on site (program director or university supervisor) who is prepared to step in and manage a difficult situation. Volunteers must not be left alone to deal with more than that for which they are trained or qualified to handle. If there is no appropriate support person on site, then the volunteer needs to change modalities to something light and simple.

These recommendations are not intended to discourage volunteers or students from working with older adults in a community group. Even professionals in psychology, counseling, and nursing have to know the limits of their competence; so too the volunteers and students have to acknowledge their proper roles with ample room to flourish within those roles.

Recommendations for All Group Leaders

Keeping up with new ideas in aging research and group programs is important for group leaders from all backgrounds. Geriatric group work is an evolving aspect of gerontology where there is ample room to develop programs that become the gold standard in future years. Sharing ideas and discovering what other group leaders are doing is important to elevate this work from mere activity to a meaningful group process.

Look for opportunities to gain specialized training in geriatric group work. Professional counselors, psychologists, and nurses can earn continuing education credits by attending programs on geriatric education. Some of these programs allow students to attend. Check with local and regional universities that have a degree in Aging Studies or Gerontology. Local professionals as well as volunteers in aging group programs can ask for permission to attend special programs or lectures. Mental Health Counselors, Clinical Social Workers, and Psychologists may be able to take a gerontology class for credit or audit to fill in the gaps that were not provided in their core degrees. Current students in colleges or universities that do not have an aging studies program may also be able to take a class in gerontology or aging studies that will transfer into their current degree programs.

Connect with a geriatric education program, research center, or treatment facility. Universities that have aging studies are likely to also have expanded continuing education programs. The National Association of Geriatric Education Centers (www.nagec.org) supports Geriatric Education Centers (GECS) nationwide as well as provides resources for gerontologists and other health care professionals who work with older adults. This group also provides advanced training for nurses, dentists, mental health professionals, and faculty who are interested in expanding their knowledge of applied gerontology within their respective fields.

Organizations like the Gerontological Society of America (GSA) offer a wealth of information and major journals in this field. GSA members have online access to journal articles. However, their flagship publications, *The Gerontologist* and the *Journal of Gerontology*, can be found at an academic library or Geriatric Education Center. The current issue of the online newsletter, *Gerontology News*, is available to members during the month of publication. Past issues can be accessed by nonmembers at http://www.geron.org/Publications/Gerontology%20 News. Online newsletters offer the advantage of getting new information out to geriatric practitioners faster than journals or books.

The National Gerontological Nursing Association provides conferences and webinars for nurses as well as external continuing education for nurses, nurse practitioners, physicians, and psychologists. This organization publishes the clinical journal, *Geriatric Nursing*.

The local Area Agency on Aging (AAOA) serves persons over age 60 and those who work with older adults. Whether volunteers, congregate living providers, faith-based organizations with adult day programs, adult day care, or professionals, all levels of care providers benefit from staying in contact with the local AAOA. To find the nearest program, look in the local phone listings or at the National Association of Area Agencies on Aging website, http://www.n4a.org/. The local AAOA maintains information on elder care facilities, transportation, and other programs that are valuable particularly to community dwelling elders and to family caregivers. A nonprofessional can get a quick review of aging issues by reading the aging topics and local issues that are most relevant to a local area by studying the AAOA website. Some of the AAOA offices are also designated as Aging and Disability Resource Centers (ADRCs). The ADRC is particularly helpful in finding the right type of transportation to community elder group programs for persons with specific disabilities.

4

GROUP LOCATION

A group of people may gather anywhere: at the mall, the student center, office break room, or basketball court. While these gatherings may be referred to in common conversation as a "group," it takes more than several people in the same place at the same time to constitute a therapeutic or structured group. Finding the right location for this type of group to meet is an extremely important factor in the success of the group.

As real estate professionals know, the key to successful property development is "location, location, location." That's equally true for geriatric group programs. The majority of geriatric groups are conducted in long term care facilities, many of which have multiple levels of care. Residential facilities with specific care plans have a responsibility to attend to various needs of the residents with programs and activities. For that reason, there are two benefits to providing group work in a full service residential setting. First, the residents are available; and second, there are spaces to conduct a group such as the activity room or community room.

Depending on the group modality, the open community rooms are not the best choice. Too much surrounding noise and movement is distracting to the group, particularly for those with hearing problems. The room must also have space to accommodate several wheelchairs if members are less mobile. A room without a door also reduces privacy and is not suitable for a group that is focusing on adjustment or depression issues.

Long Term Care/Nursing Homes

Residents in long term care or nursing homes who are cognitively aware can be ready to move away from the four walls of their rooms into a different location. Even those who walk or are transported to the "day room" can feel lost in the crowd of people sitting around watching television or out in the hallway watching staff walk back and forth. Coming to a group where each resident gets personal attention in an environment makes the residential facility less like what one resident described to me as "like spending the day in a bus terminal while life goes past."

Unlike the smaller space of a dementia unit dining room, the congregate dining room for a long term care facility may resemble a restaurant. Here the residents may chat at their tables and never have contact with other residents on the other side of the room. The perception that residents have of this large room as well as the size makes it unsuitable for groups. Be aware that the director may prefer to have the geriatric group and several other activities occurring simultaneously in different corners of the large dining room, but this is not suitable for GSE groups. Politely resist that suggestion. The noise and distractions of the other activities will compromise the rapport building, cohesion, and actual work of the group. Keep in mind that you are the advocate for the geriatric group, seeking a location that gives them the greatest benefit. It may not please housekeeping to have another room in use, but that is not your problem. Locating a comfortable, cozy, and private space for the group is your priority.

Look for a family living room area, conference room, or even a chapel. This group needs to have a closed space where the hallway sounds and external traffic is diminished. If there is furniture in the room, such as a conference room, think about whether the room can be used as it is currently staged or if it needs to be arranged. Can you get permission for the director to move aside part of the conference table or rearrange side chairs so that residents in wheelchairs have easy access? How will you arrange the existing furniture to create a circle or half circle for the group so that everyone can see and hear each other?

Consider lighting in the group room. If possible, turn off the institutional fluorescent ceiling lights. This is harsh lighting and does not give the impression of visiting with friends in a living room. Look for side lighting options, and make certain it is bright enough for safe movement. For activities that require more light, the overhead lights can be used. Ask the group for their opinion on which lighting style they prefer.

If most of the group members require wheelchair transport, ask the director how that can be most efficiently accomplished. Unless the geriatric group is on the schedule with enough advance time for staff members to transport residents, half of the group time will be over before the entire group arrives. Finding a time for group when there is time for staff to help with transport is another significant scheduling issue. Also ask the director if the GSE group leader or student volunteer is allowed to move residents in wheelchairs. Typically, for liability reasons, only staff is allowed to handle the movement of wheelchairs. If that is the case, respect the rule. If group leaders are allowed to participate in wheelchair transport, have the nursing director demonstrate the proper procedure and make certain that each GSE group leader has professional liability insurance that covers this action. Generally speaking, unless the GSE group leader is a nurse or other staff member at the facility, do not expect professional liability for usual and customary duties of psychotherapy or psychology to cover resident transport. This seems so simple, yet it can turn complicated quickly.

Before bringing in art materials or anything that could be messy, get permission of the director. If the modality calls for music, make certain that the CD player is either battery powered or that the electric cord is not in the path of any resident who could trip and fall. The best way to bring display materials is to use things that are on a portable easel or handheld. If possible, request a locker at the facility for basic group materials or ask permission to bring a small locking cabinet. Over time this is much easier than loading and unloading group supplies from the car for every group.

Long Term Care/Dementia Units

Groups for cognitively impaired residents need to be located within the dementia unit. Although many of the cognitively impaired residents may be ambulatory, these residents are often at high risk for wandering, which sends the group leader on unplanned sprints in pursuit.

Attempting to move several cognitively impaired residents is a one-on-one process so without several staff members to assist, this takes up time that could better be spent in group process.

As much at it confounds newcomers working with dementia patients, these cognitively impaired residents have a sense of belonging on their unit and become agitated or resistant when they are moved in another area of the facility. The better designed dementia units have individual dining room areas within each unit that do not require leaving for a larger communal dining area. This dining room can be a useful space for some group activities. These in-unit dining areas are smaller, which makes it easier for a group to gather in one section, and there is likely a door to close off the dining area from the hallway. The facility staff may be more willing to allow group members to have juice and snacks during group if limited to the dining room, and the group time does not interfere with set-up for the next food service.

A small room with a window and door (to reduce hallway distractions) is usually more comfortable for cognitively impaired residents. Dementia units in better quality facilities have a living room type of space for residents to gather or for family visits that can be reserved during the day for group. Don't be surprised if a non-group member wanders in or a group member leaves unexpectedly. Overall, in the GSE experience, there was less wandering, disruption, or inattention when the cognitively impaired groups were held inside the dementia unit rather than attempting to transport members to an activity room in another area of the facility. If there is any transport involved, even within the unit area, keep in mind the admonitions explained in the prior section. Any movement of residents, regardless of cognitive status, involves risk and ultimately professional and personal liability.

Unexpected location changes test the group leader's adaptability. During the remodeling of a dementia unit, the living room was closed to the GSE group for several weeks. This inability to enter the room already stirred up the residents. The group leader's only option for staying on the unit was to get permission to create a circle of chairs at the end of a hallway. A staff member and the group leader did the chair arrangement before gathering the group members to reduce distractions. To the leader's amazement, this less-than-desirable location worked better than the previous week's attempt to move residents to another unit for group. Having a choice of several locations may work well for cognitively aware group members but not for the cognitively impaired ones. Regardless of the location that the group leader prefers, what matters is how well it works for the group. Stay flexible!

Assisted Living Facilities

Residents in assisted living vary in their levels of mobility and awareness. Assisted living facilities may have defined space for residents based on the level of care they require. Within one facility may be a floor of residents or a grouping of cottages that enjoy congregate dining and have medication reminders but are otherwise ambulatory and alert. Some of these residents may still have their cars and periodically leave the facility for shopping and social events. Another floor within a contained building may have residents who require more assistance with activities of daily living such as bathing, dressing, medication, and meals. Less mobile residents do not leave the facility except for specified appointments or to visit family.

The GSE group leader needs to know the level of mobility, independence, and autonomy of the potential group members. Residents who are more mobile may not be as faithful attendees of group as those who remain in the facility. If the facility has regular outings for the active residents such as bus to the grocery, movies, shopping or community events, then the GSE groups will compete with time on the schedule. Arranging the group times and dates for more mobile residents can be done first, then fill in the times for less mobile residents.

A full service elder community may have independent living apartments, assisted living, and long term care on the same campus. This concept is particularly popular for older couples who need different levels of care. One spouse can remain in the apartment and be within walking distance from the other spouse who is in long term care. GSE groups that are part of this type of community have to adapt modalities to the different needs and participation levels of each group. Even within an assisted living, if there are different levels of care needs, then it is preferable not to mix the group members.

Look for a family living room space or smaller, closed community room where the group can have dedicated space. While there may not be as much wandering in assisted living, there are also more cognitively aware residents who could be listening to the group. Each group needs to feel that what is said in group is private. If group members feel that other residents are being nosey, they will stop communicating or refuse to attend group. While you may think this is overreacting, consider that an assisted living facility can be like a college dormitory where everybody wants to mind each other's business and lives in close proximity. Communal living seems to have that effect on some people, which is compounded because residents in assisted living have less outside contact or interaction.

For assisted living residents who are independently mobile or only require a walker or cane for support, the options are often greater for finding a private group room. These residents may be able to comfortably sit in one of the family living rooms or adapt to a conference room. Ideally the conference room is large enough to pull the chairs away from the table and form a circle. If not, it can still work by gathering the group closely at one end of the table. When the leader makes this extra effort to find a suitable, private group room, the group members get an emotional lift and enjoy the oasis from the routine that group provides.

Adult Day Care

An adult day care may be arranged within a nursing home, adjacent to an assisted living facility, or as a free-standing program that is a business or service of a community nonprofit program. Like assisted living, adult day care can be targeted to specific populations or to those with special needs. While a population of varied skills and cognitive abilities may be legal in a given area, it is not the best environment for GSE groups unless the group members can be matched to the modalities that suit their level of functioning.

An adult day care is a limited service facility and as such usually has a more open room concept with a dining space, or it conducts all activities in one large room. A free-standing adult day care is only open during weekdays with hours convenient for family caregivers who also have full-time jobs. As a result, these facilities tend to have fewer, if any, locations for group.

If the adult day care is part of a long term care or assisted living facility, then look for those spaces within the larger building that work best for the group. Attempting to conduct a group in a corner of the larger adult care open concept room has the same problem as trying to work in a communal dining room. A conference room may be the only option at a smaller adult day care, and it's worth making the effort to adapt.

Community Centers

Community centers are a valued part of city or county recreation programs. Some may be designated as centers for older adults who also have congregate dining during weekdays. Other community centers are privately funded and sponsored by a charitable organization like Neighborly Senior Centers, Elder Help, Jewish Community Center, Catholic Social Services, or other centers supported by private foundations.

Some community centers are part of a larger recreation center. Those that are faith based are on the campus of the sponsoring organization, and others are free-standing facilities. The larger community centers have more flexibility in space arrangement or various smaller rooms suitable for geriatric groups. Find the room that is a comfortable fit for a small group and not too far from the main activities hub of the community center. The mobility of group members is a major consideration in choosing a group room. Community centers are not required to have the number of staff or enough who are trained in transport to make it easy to get less mobile group members from the main rooms to a group room. The group leader may be a student or volunteer who has to depend on other volunteers to escort less mobile participants to the group room. The same warnings about assisting with transport apply here as already stated for long term care.

During congregate dining or other times when there is a large gathering at the community center, ask the coordinator for time to give a short, enthusiastic comment about the geriatric groups. Other attendees may not know what this group is about or whether they might be interested. Keep the comments brief and non-therapeutic. If it sounds like drudgery or "counseling," the older participants will not want to join. Make it personal as if you could hardly wait to let them in on the best kept secret in the community center. If you have a group member who can be brief and keep it upbeat, invite that person to be a testimony of the value he or she finds in the group.

Staff Cooperation

Even if the geriatric group is a self-contained program with its own leaders and materials, the GSE group is not an island within the facility. The attitudes of nursing and patient care staff, adult day care workers, or volunteers in community centers can make or break this group program. Securing the approval for GSE groups from the director or supervisor of the facility is only the first step. Before making the final commitment to bring groups into any type of facility, meet with the primary staff and present the group concept. Watch their faces during the presentation and while you answer questions. The look of disdain, particularly from staff in a long term care facility, is not necessarily in opposition to the groups but rather a nonverbal groan over still another schedule to meet in an already busy daily care agenda. In long term care and assisted living, the staff are the people on whom you depend to have the group members dressed, fed and ready to transport to group. Without their cooperation, the group program will fail miserably.

In one situation, GSE leaders began developing a relationship with the facility staff weeks before groups started. As licensed professionals, the initial GSE leaders were able to present in-service training on topics that the staff appreciated, such as communication strategies for working with cognitively impaired elders, the role of groups for reducing social isolation in care facility residents, and how to deal with caregiver burnout. The GSE leaders gave interactive presentations to stimulate discussion with the staff and build rapport rather than showing up like the experts ready to reform and issue orders. This time spent "paying it forward" to the staff demonstrated that we wanted to be part of the treatment team and partner with them to support the residents. The leaders also lived up to the agreement to participate in treatment team meetings and remained available by phone or appointment to visit with the group members' family and primary care physicians.

The group leaders set quarterly meetings with the facility's social services director to discuss advance scheduling. Several times during the year, such as Christmas holidays, there were unusual demands on space and time with other special programs. Knowing in advance about these interruptions and space changes helped the leaders to avoid schedule conflicts and reduced frustrations on both sides.

Maintaining regular contact with the nursing director and each unit supervisor, group leaders asked for their support in impressing upon the staff the importance of regular group attendance. To be effective, geriatric groups could not be treated the same as an optional drop-in anytime to hear the local scout troop sing event. As staff began to see the benefits of regular group participation, they made extra efforts to arrange outside medical and dental appointments as well as showers and personal care during times that did not conflict with the group schedule.

In short, GSE leaders gave cooperation and respect to the facility staff and received the same in return. As a result of establishing a professional relationship where positive regard was given to staff at all levels from administrator to aides, the group leaders had minimal problems with attendance, as participants were usually ready on time and transported as needed to group.

The same cooperative approach works with community groups and adult day care. Find out what the staff does in a typical day. Look at the schedule. Think about how you would manage the logistics that are necessary to make this program work. Then consider adding a group program. Looking at this from the facility staff's or volunteers' viewpoint can make it easier to plan a win–win strategy.

5

FUNDING FOR GERIATRIC GROUPS

Motivation is what gets you started. Habit is what keeps you going.

Jim Rohn

In 1965, President Lyndon Johnson signed the law implementing Medicare for persons over age 65 and Medicaid for the indigent, opening the door for greater health care services to older adults. For decades since, Medicare has operated in the shadow of the grim reaper, with predictions of financial collapse looming ever closer to reality. Various efforts to control rising Medicare costs have been tried since the early concerns over increased patient usage and decreasing resources arose. Both beneficiaries (patients) and providers (physicians and others) have been targets of political battles, cost containment, and benefits changes. Medicare's checkered past as it relates to mental health providers is too lengthy and intricate to relate in this chapter. Since Medicare and other proposals for a national health care system are batted around frequently, it's difficult to say what system might be in place next quarter or next year.

At the time of this writing, Medicare is the major payer for geriatric group work with some additional funding from supplemental insurance policies or Medicaid. This is the typical funding process as long as the type of group work you provide meets Medicare guidelines and group leaders are appropriately licensed providers to render those services. As for any other rules and guidelines, those seem to have the same longevity as bank business signs.

How to Consistently Get Paid

Experience is a treacherous yet profound teacher. For geriatric groups in long term care, assisted living, or other locations, the groups may be suitable for reimbursement as therapy. Regardless of the system in place for reimbursement, avoid expensive mistakes and improve payment rates by following these tips:

1. Attend a regional Medicare provider seminar before launching the group program. Keep in mind that Medicare (or whatever system is in place) is influenced by politics, which can lead to sudden, dramatic changes in reimbursement. Don't be surprised to discover that a group code approved last month is no longer viable this month. When attending the provider seminar, meet and get business cards from as many of the provider relations staff as possible. These are people with whom you will interact for billing questions and other issues. Time spent attending provider meetings is time well spent for gathering information and making contacts.

2. Obtain all the paperwork needed before admitting a new member into group. Create a checklist of which card, identification, and so forth are needed.

3. Double-check intake forms and other group information to properly conform to HIPPA or other existing requirements that safeguard client information.

4. Make sure you understand all the blanks, boxes, and lines of a billing form before submitting. Correcting mistakes means delayed, possibly disapproved payment.

5. Keep copies of everything sent to Medicare or other insurance carriers. Electronic records are easier to store than paper. Paper records can be scanned, but that's time consuming. Have every record coded in such a way for quick retrieval, whether paper or electronic.

6. Document all treatment contacts, methods, and results. The rule is if you can't prove it, don't bill for it.

7. Coordinate with the long term care or assisted care treatment team as part of group modality planning. This is an additional justification for the work if questioned.

8. Set up a random check procedure for all claims generated for your groups. Assign a person who does not regularly input the claims to proofread and review. Do this weekly for at least three months until the process is running smoothly. Thereafter, do spot checks with complete review of randomly selected weeks at least quarterly. If you contract with a billing service, ask about their procedure for reviews and checks.

9. Establish a reminder system with a paper or electronic calendar that flags overdue payments from Medicare or other payment sources. Don't let these slip by. The payers are not in a hurry to part with the money. When a Medicare Update bulletin arrives, read it immediately! New information that affects your payments is announced in the bulletin and as a provider, you are expected to know this information and follow any new procedures.

ion for treatment plan on the work that the group does. If possible, use the
same note for both facility chart and group treatment notes to save time.

Getting paid for geriatric group work under Medicare or other third-party
payers is a moving target. The changes in health care reimbursement seem to be
particularly challenging for mental health services. Take time to set up the process,
billing system, and monitoring. After that, move forward with the more exciting business of providing innovative, interactive geriatric groups to older adults
whose lives are enriched by this work.

Alternative Funding for Geriatric Groups

Bringing your own basket to a class reunion picnic is one thing, but finding your
own funding for group work? Yes, it's possible and becoming an enticing option
for four basic reasons:

1. Not all group leaders who are suitable for certain types of group work qualify
   as Medicare or other insurance providers.
2. Services covered today under Medicare, Medicaid, and Medigap may be reduced or eliminated tomorrow.
3. Cost-containment efforts may limit types of group work to brief psychotherapy for even severe diagnostic categories and refuse to pay for creative
   modalities that deal with adjustment, pain, life span crises, and grief.
4. The tidal wave of Baby Boomers reaching retirement age means that early in
   the 21st century there will be far more geriatric patients in need of services
   than money to pay for those services, according even to optimistic estimates
   of the Medicare and Medicaid systems.

With these factors in mind, don't give up. The ideas that follow are to motivate
you to discover opportunities for developing a geriatric group program. In so
doing, group leaders become partners with the local community in the delivery
of elder services.

Nonprofit Organizations

The most visible nonprofit local service organizations are faith-based organizations,
churches, community centers, and senior citizen centers. Look over the bulletins
of several large local faith-based organizations that have an active senior adult
program. Many community centers also plan social, recreational, and exercise activities for senior adults during the midday hours when their other populations—
working adults and children—are not prime users of the facility. Naturally, senior
citizen centers are targeted to meet a full spectrum of needs for elders.

Geriatric group programs can be tailored to fit the needs of participants in any of the existing organizations. Elders are already attracted to these facilities, so there is some built-in potential for group membership. These organizations have a loyal membership, identity in the community, methods of promoting their programs (i.e., bulletins, newsletters, websites, etc.), multipurpose building space, and other valuable connections. A well-planned, multimodal geriatric group brings a fresh approach to a schedule that is often filled with traditional arts and crafts or coffee clubs. Don't be shy about reminding the center director that geriatric groups can generate new interest in the overall program by offering something that meets an immediate need. For example, short-term grief groups, particularly near holidays, may motivate newcomers to attend for this purpose and discover that there are other activities at the center that they may attend. This is a win–win situation: The elders win by finding new opportunities to socialize and learn, and the center wins with greater usage and the potential to gain new members.

The group program might be designed with two tracks: a closed group series for five weeks on art and expression or phototherapy and several alternating open groups. Many community centers have a season or semester calendar similar to school with fall, winter, spring, and summer sessions. Plan programs accordingly.

Set a minimum enrollment number for closed groups, and prepare adequate materials. As part of the nonprofit organization's program schedule, geriatric groups gain an implied endorsement of that organization, so be certain you want to share their reputation and population.

Research Grants

Grants are plentiful; grants are impossible to get—both are true, depending on the requirements and the strength of the proposed program. What is common is that the bigger the bucks, the tougher the competition. Fortunately, that's not a major issue for the geriatric group program that can operate with thousands, not millions. Attracting the interest of multinational corporations and national agencies is less significant than finding support from regional corporations and state agencies. Think medium to small. Search for supplemental funding for local geriatric group work, not a full staff and a limo.

The fine art of grant seeking and writing is the subject of many books and is too extensive to include here. Begin by investing in attending a weekend seminar or local evening college course on grant writing. Next, talk with local community centers, senior centers, or Area Offices on Aging about the group leaders' desire to find additional support for geriatric groups as well as contribute to research in the field.

Find the nearest university with a graduate program in gerontology, counseling, or social work. Universities are virtual heat-seeking missiles for grants. So what do you have to offer them? Geriatric groups are another training site for students as coleaders or assistants.

Spend time in the library or on Internet sources scouting notices and directories of grants. Look for such titles as elderly health services, gerontology and mental health, or social services. Several grant directories are listed in the resources at the end of this book.

Before deciding to pursue larger research grants, be certain that you have the desire and ability to produce a quality study that will genuinely enhance the profession of gerontology. Grants are not the answer to support an otherwise ineffective and unsuccessful geriatric program.

Community Grants

Making the city, county, and region a better place to live is everybody's business, particularly key employers. The trend toward visibly investing back into the local area is catching on in corporations of all sizes. From the pledge to clean up a highway mile to sponsorship of wheelchair sporting events, local companies are following the corporate giants in doing good works. Group work is another form of good work for the community.

Ask the larger local and regional corporations if they have mini-grants for investment in specialized programs to serve their community. Corporations, particularly if they profit from offering products to elders, may want the positive image of supporting a community elder service. Civic and service clubs underwrite various local projects. If you are primarily seeking scholarship money for elders who cannot afford to attend geriatric groups in a community setting, then several smaller grants may be sufficient.

Adult Day Care

Elders are living longer at a time when custodial care costs are skyrocketing. Moving in with adult children or other family members is one choice that reduces expenses but leaves the elder at home alone during the day while younger adults are at work. Filling the gap in care for these elders is adult day care. To make this care feasible for working adult children, many elder day cares open early and close late to conform to work hours, similar to children's day care.

Like their youthful counterparts, elders may spend up to 10 hours in adult day care. Meaningful activity is important during these most productive hours of an elder's day. With many blocks of time to fill, multimodal geriatric groups are a welcome alternative for the participants and the weary staff. Further ideas for including group work under contract to the day care are presented in the next section on fees. Adult day care is more advanced in some areas than others. Visit or write to these programs in other cities to inquire about their daily schedules. Demonstrate your knowledge of this subject and your program plan when you present geriatric groups to an adult day care director.

Determining Your Fees

Many group leaders have difficulty asking for payment. Persons who choose the helping professions are notoriously reluctant collection agents. However, meeting the needs in the largely underserved elder population will not happen unless group leaders get paid for their work.

Group leaders who are appropriately licensed and qualify as Medicare and insurance providers have payment guidelines to use in setting fees. Otherwise, set fees for the group that are reasonable within your community, based on an informal survey of prices. There is a financial advantage in working with nonprofit organizations or adult day care where greater latitude is given to use an organization's facility and its promotional publication with less overhead and expenses for the group program.

Many community recreation centers have fee-based programs such as genealogy, woodworking, and breakfast club. Their members are accustomed to paying to participate. Geriatric group fees can be within a reasonable range, based on what type of groups are offered. Closed groups with more focus and preparation of the activities command higher per-group (or session) fees than open groups. Certain types of closed groups (such as Alzheimer's groups) work best with a smaller group and a coleader. Without the Medicare limit on group size, a well-trained leader can, for example, manage a dozen higher functioning members in a bibliotherapy or humor group.

For any church or faith-based organization that shows interest in its senior adults, geriatric groups are a natural extension of outreach. The easiest way to begin is to schedule groups within or adjacent to an existing senior adult program. A typical format for senior adult programs is a full weekday morning of activities that occurs weekly or biweekly. Another way to make the session more open to all interested seniors is to recommend that the organization offer some scholarship or underwriting assistance for members to attend your groups. Geriatric groups enhance the senior adult ministry, which can offer some assistance in payment for disadvantaged elders to participate.

Senior citizen centers and adult day care are fully dedicated to elders, so every day demands an agenda of stimulating activities, like a GSE-style geriatric group program! Talk with the director to learn about his or her needs. You may also discover that the senior center has several funding sources from donations, cities, clubs, and other community support. The senior center may have access to funds to underwrite participation in group for some needy elders. Considering the lengthy hours of operation for many adult day care centers, multimodal geriatric groups are a productive addition to long hours for elders away from their homes. Remind the day care director that elders involved in satisfying pursuits, discovering things about themselves, and finding appreciative outlets for their reminiscences, complain far less and are more cooperative. Payment in this scenario is a type of contract work between the day care and geriatric group program to deliver a certain number of groups or for a stated amount of time. Be careful about accepting a per-client, per-group fee only, or other performance-oriented fees. Set a fee by the type of service rendered and for a maximum number of participants. For example, a leader may charge a per-group hourly rate to conduct a remotivation group for 8–10 participants, three times weekly. Whatever financial incentives are offered, pay is better for staying four hours at one location than for working two hours at two locations with unpaid travel time between sites.

Income Tax Considerations

Are you an independent contractor just because you have a contract with a center to provide geriatric group work? The answer is maybe. The way to determine the accurate answer to the satisfaction of the Internal Revenue Service is to pass the "test" found in IRS Publication 937, Employment Taxes. Pay attention to all of the factors required to define the difference between an employee and independent contractor. Remaining an independent contractor can be in both your best interest and that of the organization where you conduct groups. Failure to meet this test can deem you an employee of the organization. Consult the IRS publication for details, and discuss any questions with a tax accountant or certified public accountant.

Survival of the Creative

In the evolution of health care, the need for geriatric services is rising at a time when costs are being trimmed. Case managers are making dozens of critical care decisions daily. Is group therapy for an elder this week more important than funds that may be needed next month for that same person's hospitalization? That's a difficult and circuitous question.

If nothing else is learned from reading this chapter, please grasp the concept that being creative in seeking funding sources and contract work opportunities for geriatric groups is a viable alternative. Take a consultation approach, and find a capable business planner or an informal group of local businesspeople who will give advice on carrying out ideas in this chapter. Working with the local Small Business Association center is another way to expand business knowledge. Take advantage of a wealth of business information and local seminars provided by the U.S. Small Business Association, a government service. Look online for the nearest SBA office (www.sba.gov), or call 1-800-827-5722 (within the continental United States).

No matter what happens with insurance and Medicare funding, the need for geriatric groups is growing as the population ages. Geriatric group programs that have mastered the art of finding creative funding alternatives will survive and blossom in the approaching era of tight third-party purse strings.

6

GROUP MODALITIES FOR THE MIND

I cannot but remember such things were, that were most precious to me.

William Shakespeare, *Macbeth*

Memories are the subject of endless songs, poems, and stories. How often do you hear people of all ages say, "I'll never forget the time. . ."? Sharing memories is an important part of human conversation. Much therapeutic emphasis in working with survivors of traumatic events is in recovering memories to resolve the distress. Equally strong is the opposing viewpoint claiming that therapists are planting false memories or improperly interpreting true memories. Setting aside both positions on this volatile issue, it does demonstrate the potentially life-changing impact of memories.

Practical Value of Reminiscence

Music legend and former Beatle (now senior adult) Paul McCartney attempted to save a message on his cell phone only to receive the warning—"memory almost full." Chances are he was not aware of many earlier messages stored in that phone: memories forgotten but not lost. In working with older adults, group leaders are frequently amazed at how a certain scent, movement, musical refrain, or conversation can trigger a memory of decades past in vivid detail. It may seem that the memory is almost full, but the brain has amazing storage potential. What we lose is the access code. As you see an older adult struggle to find the right words or to finish a conversation, think of how you feel when you can't access an online account because the password is incorrect. By the way, Sir Paul was not frustrated but rather inspired by his cell phone problem and used that message "memory almost full" as the title of his 2007 album.

Reminiscence as a doorway to the mind and its rich memory storage has a long-standing use in group work and individual therapy with older adults. Whether the memory is easily accessed or aging and memory impairment makes it harder to connect with memories, reminiscence can be the key.

Therapists, nurses, or family caregivers may have the initial reaction to tune out each time Grandma repeats the same story. Rather than bemoan the repetition, realize that this memory can be used to help her deal better with present circumstances. This is the essence of reminiscence, which can be engaged in group or individual work with senior adults. Reminiscence is a technique for using an elder's natural desire to talk about "the good old days" as a means of recalling past strengths and contentment to enhance coping in the present. Minardi and Hayes (2003) remind readers that while "reminiscence is undertaken by people in most age groups," according to Pasupathi and Carstensen (2003), "older adults experience social reminiscing as more emotionally positive and less emotionally negative than do younger adults" (p. 431).

Reminiscence to the untrained may seem useless or distracting from present concerns. Sadly, the repetition of or even obsession with certain stories from the past too often is met with a caregiver's response of frustration or anger at what is incorrectly perceived as losing touch with the present. Such a rush to judgment dismisses the value of what can be learned from those memories. Group leaders must refrain from such destructive responses. As geriatric group members participate in reminiscence, they discover that who they were remains a vital part of who they are today. They may look different in the mirror, but in their heart and mind they are the same.

Remembering past events can be as comforting to senior adults as warm cocoa on a chilly winter morning. The positive feelings that memories can evoke are the subject of an entire magazine, *Reminisce*, which is filled with stories, photos, humor, and homespun advice. Its readers are the source of the material featured in this publication. Imagine how many untapped reminiscences lie waiting to be discovered in geriatric groups. Any practitioner with experience in conducting reminiscence groups knows what it is like to be amazed at the wealth of experiences and living history represented by group members.

In the therapeutic literature, reminiscence is frequently subdivided into simple reminiscence and life review. Butler's (1963) groundbreaking article on life review laid the foundation for the value of reminiscence as a way to reflect upon and summarize the life span of an individual. Butler challenged the mind-set of health professionals who were quick to dismiss senior adult reminiscences as a sign of them losing their faculties rather than of their engaging in an adaptive process of aging. Later articles by Kaminsky (1984), Birren (1987), and Tobin and Gustafson (1987) supported Butler's belief about the benefits of reminiscence. Webster (1999) added the element of looking at various causal factors in life events that can add perspective to life review. Hyden and Orulv (2009) found that the retelling of stories even when not well organized by time and place has value for persons with dementia. Within these stories are the memories that in small ways allow the individual to connect with his or her identity.

LoGerfo (1980–1981) described three distinct types of reminiscence: informative, evaluative, and obsessive. The evaluative type is most like Butler's (1963) life review. Informative reminiscence is the timeless tradition of sharing stories and passing along family history. Obsessive reminiscence is rumination filled with guilt, fear, mourning, or self-deprecating beliefs that need resolution more than repetition. Inexperienced group leaders are known to allow these pity parties of obsessive reminiscence to dampen the group's effectiveness and fail to address the real needs of the distraught participants.

Sherman and Havinghurst (1970) suggested that an increased desire to recall memories correlates with aging. Acting on this desire enhances adjustment, self-acceptance, and ego strength, according to Havinghurst and Glasser (1972). Lewis and Butler (1974) showed how memories can have psychotherapeutic impact in improving self-worth and perspective by reliving past events through the eyes of others. Scogin, Welsh, Hanson, Stump, and Coates (2005) compared studies of reminiscence therapy and found that the majority provided evidence-based support for the efficacy of reminiscence. Rather than use further space to detail the many early articles on reminiscence and life review, readers are referred to Watt and Wong (1991), who prepared an excellent taxonomy on this subject that is particularly suitable to provide background on the early development of reminiscence for students, researchers, and group leaders in training. Webster, Bohlmeijer, and Westerhof (2010) took a leap forward in their comprehensive article on "Mapping the Future of Reminiscence."

Research that was useful in formation of GSE's reminiscence module expanded on areas or new applications of this technique. Lowenthal and Marrazzo (1990) developed "milestoning" to recapture positive memories that can balance present distressing circumstances or being stuck in negative memories. Milestoning does not aim at the full spectrum of positive and negative experiences as does traditional life review. Thus, the milestoning approach is in harmony with the GSE's use of reminiscence to recall past strengths and contentment as a means to enhance coping in the present.

Wallace (1992) placed a positive emphasis on life review by using narrative interviews. The narrative focus has beneficial offspring in other areas of psychology and mental health such as personality (Hooker & McAdams, 2003), personal development (McLean, Pasupathi, & Pals, 2007), and psychotherapy (McLeod, 1996; White, 2007). Webster (2001, 2003) continued to develop the narrative approach to reminiscence as a significant aspect of autobiographical memory in older adults. McAdams (2005) further emphasized the value of autobiographical storytelling as a way for the older adult to sense continuity of self across the years.

GSE group leaders frequently use narrative-oriented techniques such as those presented later in this chapter. When approached from a positive slant, life review can be guided to sidestep traumatic events and steer away from obsessive memories, both of which are counterproductive for older adults for whom coping and life satisfaction are more significant than making changes. By remaining with the positive or life-affirming memories, group can be facilitated by a variety of leaders including volunteers or paraprofessionals. More intense life review techniques that may evoke abreactions and catharsis are best managed by experienced professionals. Selecting a group leader for life review demands serious consideration and consultation with a psychiatrist, psychologist, or other appropriately licensed and qualified professional.

Categories of Reminiscence and Life Review

Both life review and basic reminiscence have branched out into a variety of subcategories within the overall concept. Although the debate remains as to whether life review and reminiscence are essentially the same or significantly different, there is no consensus. This author agrees with Merriam (1989) that these techniques, although similar, are qualitatively and structurally different. Webster and Haight (1995) supported this distinction by defining reminiscence as highly spontaneous, with little structure, as compared with life review, which is more structured and comprehensive.

TABLE 6.1 Examples of Life Review Techniques

Authors	Approach
Meyerhoff & Tufte (1975)	Weekly life review classes
Koch (1977)	Poetry and expressive arts
Edinberg (1985)	Music, scents, images, and items
Hately (1985)	Spiritual themes in life history
Birren (1987)	Guided autobiography in group
Sweeny (1990)	Early recollections within an Adlerian context
Crose (1990)	Gestalt techniques
Waters & Goodman (1990)	Guided imagery, life review, autobiographies, systematic interviews
Kartman (1991)	Music of holidays, religious tradition, or by popular music of a certain time period
Birren & Cochran (2001)	Guided by a life review facilitator or therapist
Peck (2001)	Explore schemas and stereotypes as influences on well-being over the life span
Kralik, Koch, Price, & Howard (2004)	Identify life history information that may provide coping strategies for dealing with chronic illness
Puentes (2004)	Life Review integrated with Cognitive Therapy
Helmeke (2006)	Spiritual Life Review
Haight & Haight (2007)	Structured Life Review with Therapeutic Listener

With life review becoming more distinct from simple reminiscence, specific techniques acknowledge the need to deal with different types of memories. Lo-Gerfo (1980–1981) made this concept clear when she differentiated among three ways to engage in reminiscence. Informative reminiscence is a pleasurable recall of favorite stories of people, places, and events that can be used to rebuild self-esteem. Evaluative reminiscence most closely resembles life review. A more structured personal history, evaluative reminiscence explores an individual's strengths and weaknesses to achieve resolution of the past and self-acceptance. Obsessive reminiscence can be prolonged grief, dissociating from the present by choosing to retreat into the past, and generally getting stuck in a counterproductive activity. Informative and evaluative approaches can be effective and used in many ways. Obsessive reminiscence requires redirection and a safe place to release negative

TABLE 6.2 Examples of Types of Reminiscences

Authors	Types of reminiscence
Kaminsky (1975)	Dreams, images, and songwriting
Kaminsky (1984)	Living history drama
Clements (1982)	Recreational reminiscence
Merriam (1989)	Simple reminiscence
Watt & Wong (1991)	Escapist reminiscence
	Instrumental reminiscence
	Integrative reminiscence
	Narrative reminiscence
	Obsessive reminiscence
	Transmissive reminiscence
Erwin (1992)	Casual—stories or free association
	Relational—important relationships
	Analytical—life review
	Defensive—uses defensive mechanisms
	Obsessive—rumination
Creanza & McWhirter (1994)	Life themes and gender issues
Meacham (1995)	First standpoint—accurate recall
	Second standpoint—discover meaning
	Third Standpoint—social construct
Wareing (2000)	Person-centered approach
McAdams et al. (2001)	Autobiographical stories
Chaudhury (2003)	Place-based Reminiscence

emotions that are more appropriate for a grief and loss group or individual therapy. Such intense release of emotional pain needed for healing is rarely desirable in aging adult groups. Here are some ideas that preceded or expanded on LoGerfo's concept.

In general, reminiscence and life review can be supported by scaffolding or providing supportive structure to the storytelling (Moore & Davis, 2002). For example, the group leader can be there to add encouragement "that was so well done," prompt "and then what happened," affective question "how did you feel after that," or affirmation "you are a brave person." The scaffolding technique not only alleviates frustrations of forgetfulness that are particularly distressing to persons with memory impairment, but also demonstrates that the leader is listening and honoring the story (Kontos, 2005).

Interactive Methods and Group Activities

So many group workbooks use "therapy speak" or generalized terms that advise the leader to "set the mood," "find a common theme," or "integrate feelings with memories." What does that really say about how to plan and run geriatric groups? Not much. In this and every group module chapter, a series of actual group activities is outlined with goals, outcomes, and equipment needed for the modality.

Leaders can use the suggested themes for a single group session or continue the theme for several sessions. A positive response from the members is the best clue to extend the theme. Don't rush to abandon a theme because it fizzles with one group or on a given day. You can also repeat the theme in future groups with some changes or additions to the material. Leaders don't have to be encyclopedic experts on every group topic. Group members have taken delight in correcting the author's faulty assumptions about fishing, gardening, and driving a tractor. They will also rush to champion what they know from experience, which is a wonderful way to get even reluctant members involved in the group.

Reminiscence Groups

Reminiscence: Favorite Vacations

Goals: Recapture feelings of pleasurable leisure time. Members consider how their worldviews were changed by travel experiences.

Process: The group leader begins by telling a brief, humorous, or unique experience that occurred during a vacation. (If you have no such personal story, read a short essay or magazine article that sets the tone.) Ask each member to recall the location of his or her favorite vacation. The leader points to the place on a globe or adds a marker (pin flag or sticker) on a map, then lets each member tell something about that vacation. The leader may prompt questions for sites, smells, sounds, weather, or people who were part of that vacation. If the group is suitable and the leader has appropriate professional training, guided imagery may be used to allow all members to feel the experience in their imaginations.

Outcomes: The best result is that members are refreshed from reexperiencing vacation or travel memories. As the locations are given, other members may recall having visited or lived in the same areas. Avoid excluding persons who have never traveled for pleasure. Encourage them to talk about whatever a unique, day-off-type experience was, even if it was riding the hay wagon into town monthly to shop. Institutionalized and community elders have so much free time that "leisure" is a burden. This group theme reminds them that leisure had a satisfying place in their lives. Leaders need to listen for clues of personal interests pursued during leisure that may, in some way, be possible to duplicate now.

Equipment list: Globe or maps. Pin flags or stickers. Essays or magazine articles about traveling or photos or pictorial travel brochures that show families, couples, and adults traveling.

Reminiscence: Lifelong Learning

Goals: Discover how much each member has learned over a life span. Identify ways that learning continues even in a restricted environment and with physical impairments. This group is better suited to higher functioning elders. Those with sight or hearing impairments or an inability to write can participate with assistance from another group member or volunteer worker.

Process: Give each group member a pen and spiral notebook or sheets of lined paper with preprinted titles in a pocket folder. The leader needs a write-on board or overhead transparency projector and boldly colored markers. Begin each session with a quote or brief writing about learning. Create a group definition of learning with some free association of words for learning. This theme easily fills four to six sessions without causing members to feel rushed and allows after-group time to think about the subject. At each session, members discuss and write their feelings and recollections about these areas: first experiences of learning in elementary school; best and worst aspects of learning during formal education; skills learned on the job or in the home; things learned through hobbies, crafts, or sports; and important lessons learned from other people. A session may carry over to the next week if needed. Also, the leader may plan a wrap-up session to discuss overall feelings about this life review exercise and insights gained by each participant.

Outcomes: learning is a sign of growth, progress, and achievement. As group members identify these elements of learning at various life stages, they find evidence of accomplishments and satisfaction. By probing for informal education experiences, even members who thought they had little education can take pride in what they have learned from living.

Equipment list: Pens, notebooks, or lined paper for each participant. Lap boards or tabletop for writing. Write-on board and boldly colored markers for the group leader.

Reminiscence: My First Car

Goals: Driving and owning a car symbolizes independence, mobility, and fun. These factors are as important to elders as to teens. As each member recalls their part in the United States' fascination with the automobile, they re-experience a sense of control that is presently lost to them.

Process: The effective introduction was reading an essay from *Reminisce* magazine in which the author told of saving to buy a used Model T, working on it, and then the pride of taking his first drive around town. Male and female group members responded with recollections of saving for and anticipating their first cars. Show photos from books or magazines with cars from the 1920s, 1930s, 1940s, and 1950s and make a game of identifying the car manufacturer. Ask members to describe what driving or owning a car meant to their sense of independence, mobility, and fun. Allow members to talk about their last car and why they ceased to drive. Wrap up the final group session on this topic with an imaginary exercise. Using a write-on board or large poster board, the leader lists each member's name and transcribes the answers to each of these questions: If you awoke tomorrow with the physical ability to drive for one week and the money to buy any car you wanted, what kind of car would you buy, and where would you drive?

Outcomes: Elders often silently mourn their loss of mobility, particularly in structured institutional care. Their generation saw dramatic changes in lifestyles related to the automobile. This topic can be both jovial and serious. Even cognitively impaired patients retain strong memories of their first cars and often can describe them in detail. A library book with reproductions of auto advertisements and slogans brought great delight, as did repetition of the manufacturers' slogans. In most geriatric groups, leaders need to redirect away from memories of auto accidents or other sad events. Work with those individuals separately outside of group.

Equipment list: Scan your public library for books on old cars and car advertisements. Model cars. Audio recordings of car commercials. Contact the local antique car club for loan of these items or to drive by with a classic car. Marker board or large poster board and boldly colored markers.

Reminiscence: Childhood Games

Goals: Games were an important part of entertainment both among children and with the family after dinner. Members recall the fun of the games and the times spent with their elders talking and bonding.

Process: Begin by talking about familiar childhood games. Invite each member to tell about his or her favorite game. The leader can prompt with questions about where, when, and with which friends or siblings these games were played. Discuss which childhood games members can still enjoy, such as checkers, dominoes, or cards. Talk about how their interest in games changed over time to such activities as board games, bridge, or chess. Relate how the ability to enjoy games and fellowship is ageless.

Outcomes: Recapturing memories of carefree evenings with family and friends shows how leisure time was prized and enjoyed. Games also bring back thoughts of spending time with childhood friends, family, and special parties.

Equipment list: Bring sample games such as jacks, dominoes, marbles, checkers, or jump rope. Ask the activity director which games are popular at the facility, and bring in samples.

Reminiscence: Birthdays

Goals: Focus on celebrating life and the individual with time for each member to reflect on which birthdays were most significant and why.

Process: This theme may be lined with a group member's birthday or on another day when the attention can be shared by all. Show and discuss the typical birthday party items and plans. Ask members to share any family traditions or ethnic customs for birthdays. Wrap a small gift box for each member. Inside place a card with a word or phrase explaining what you (the leader) wish for each member. Personal wish cards need to match the individual, such as joy, patience, laughter, or self-expression. Allow each member time to respond if he or she chooses. With prior approval from the nursing staff (or physicians), have traditional treats. Close the group by sharing a birthday cake. Put lots of candles on it and sing "Happy Birthday" to the group. This theme may also be repeated on an anniversary date of the group.

Outcomes: Less cohesive groups and cognitively impaired groups will benefit more from keeping this a lighthearted event. Groups dealing with adjustment issues can find comfort in celebrating their lives rather than taking a negative view of aging. Leaders must be aware of the reactions of severely depressed members who may fixate on a bad experience. Try to encourage recalling any pleasant birthday memory—if not their own, then those of their children, family, or friends. The overall purpose is to recall those times when aging was a desirable event, and significant others celebrated their existence.

Equipment list: Birthday cake. If real cake is not allowed, there are fake cakes made from candles or fabric. Party hats and favors. Festive napkins and paper cups. A history of birthday parties or ethnic parties book from the library. Small, wrapped gift boxes with personal wish cards inside.

Reminiscence: Seasons of the Year

Goals: The changing of seasons has many meanings according to each individual's experiences. This aging cycle of nature becomes a metaphor for the life cycle, which is safer to discuss than human mortality, yet allows expression of feelings.

Process: This theme can be used quarterly at the beginning of each season or as an overview of all seasons. If all members have adequate dexterity, ask them to make a basic drawing of their favorite season. In presenting the pictures of the group, encourage the artist to talk about the objects, scene, or choice of color and why it represents a certain season. Ask members what seasonal activities they recall doing during a certain season as children and as adults. Those who grew up on farms will have different memories than those who grew up in the city. Talk about traditional events that each person associates with a certain season, such as fall hayrides and harvest parties, snow and sledding in winter, first flowers of spring, and trips to the beach in the summer. Encourage vivid word pictures for the enjoyment of everyone. If the group seems ready for a deeper level, the leader introduces discussion about the planting, growing, harvesting, and completion of crops or flowers and how this relates to stages of life.

Outcomes: Seasons are about change and transition. The leader and group members can take this topic to a variety of levels depending on the group's capability and interest.

Equipment list: Color photos or posters that depict seasons. Local travel agents and elementary school teachers will have a wealth of seasonal material to loan. Bring typical seasonal items such as knitted gloves and hats, fall leaves, spring flowers, or a beach ball.

Reminiscence: The Kitchen

Goals: Stimulate memories of mothers and grandmothers, shared times around the table at meals, and times when food was a source of pleasure.

Process: As an elder woman shared, "The kitchen was the warmest place, not just because it had the big stove, but because the whole family gathered there." The kitchen is where many important mother-child interactions occurred. Ask each member to describe his or her favorite kitchen memory as a child. Who was there? What foods were cooking? What kitchen chore did they have? In later sessions, focus on the kitchen in each person's first home (after marriage or moving away from the family). If possible, locate a replica of an old appliance catalog. Read the descriptions of the kitchen products that were "new" 40 years ago. What was the most important modern appliance bought for their new kitchen? What do they think about frozen dinners, microwave ovens, and other devices that reduce the family's time together in the kitchen and at meals?

Outcomes: This home and hearth theme branches out in several directions from nostalgia to humor to memories of the family of origin. Any of these directions can provide a stimulating group discussion.

Equipment list: Look in the library section on historic homes and older editions of kitchen design for photos of earlier kitchens. A replica of an old appliance catalog (available at bookstores and some libraries). Bring models or dollhouse replicas of potbelly stoves, wringer washers, and newer stoves. Art paper and crayons or washable markers for writing.

Reminiscence: Old Spices: Senses, Smells, and Memories

Developed with Katrina Brown.

Goals: The olfactory senses are closest to the frontal lobe of the brain, thereby eliciting memories through popular smells of the past. A group member may have a quicker recall of a particular memory resulting in informative reminiscence through smell.

Process: The group leader will find pictures of old labels of certain scents such as Old Spice for Men™, Chanel No. 5™ for women, or rose and lavender water. An easy option is to bring homemade scents in different categories such as baking scents from candles like cookie, gingerbread, pumpkins, and cinnamon.

The group leader can pass scents around to start the conversation that engages memory and sensory awareness of feelings associated with the smells. Ask questions about remembering a family member that wore the scent, or what did your mother's house smell like when she was baking?

Outcome: Smells may bypass even confusion in memory access experienced by persons with dementia and connect with memories recorded on a sensory level. Generally, the positive smells (cooking, outdoors, and personal care) bring positive memories that the group can share.

Equipment list: The group leader will make sure all scents brought are in safe containers and easy to handle. Another option is to have small plastic cups with a cotton ball in each cup. Place a drop of scent on the cotton so it can be passed easily and not become messy if dropped.

Reminiscence: Textiles and Textures of the Time

Developed with Katrina Brown.

Goal: Through the sense of touch, bring to mind feelings starting as early as the memories of soft skin and the flower petal scent a child notices when held by its mother. The ultimate goal is for informative and evaluative reminiscence of life skills, activities, and meaningful work from which there can be mood elevation and recall of past strengths.

Process: For older adults, working hard with their hands was honest labor and part of survival during difficult economic times. The group leader needs to research popular fabrics of the era, which were predominately natural ones. Old sewing books are a great resource for this information.

Outcomes: What they wore, what they used in work, and what was part of their home are familiar textures that lead to sharing memories. Some group members will respond to the design or the style of the garment. For others, the touching of the texture will be the key to relating to feelings of another time and place.

Equipment list: In addition to the fabric squares, search thrift stores for old coats, aprons, wedding gowns, and uniforms of various types of work and military. The old garment finds may be shown in whole form as a way to prompt recall of occupations, special events, and military service.

Reminiscence: Family Genogram

Goals: Constructing a genogram is a simple overview of an individual's relationships and family heritage. This project celebrates continuity of life and the individual's role in the life chain. From this glimpse of the past, behavior patterns and family roles emerge that may be therapeutically significant in the here and now.

Process: The leader explains the concept of the genogram and shows several examples of well-known families in history. Focus attention on people, relationships, major events, and interesting or unusual information about people. Using a three-generation (middle) genogram, chart their parental generation as the first generation and children or nieces and nephews as the third generation. This variation from the typical genogram process makes information retrieval easier and gives useful feedback on patients' relationships with adult children. To avoid frustration and memory blocks, eliminate dates. Divide the project into stages prepared during each group: introduce the topic; fill in the list of family names and relationship; fill in group members' generation, then add their parents' and children's generations; write in something special for each person if possible; list each person's occupation or hobby; and, finally, draw lines to indicate the nature of the relationships (close, conflicting, etc.) at a closing session, and then invite each member to present his or her own genogram to the group and discuss the most influential people in his or her life. The leader can make a transparency copy of each genogram for presentation on the overhead projector (larger and easier to read).

Outcomes: Genograms separate fact from fable by showing relationships in a concrete form. This method stimulates reassuring memories and shows unfinished business. What is learned about family patterns of scapegoating, dependency, and learned helplessness can be important in coping with present circumstances. A psychotherapist or psychologist as leader can choose to work with these intense feelings toward positive resolution. A leader with less training is advised to keep this theme on a lighter level and refer any members who are stuck in the emotional process for psychotherapy. Some of the therapeutic outcomes of genograms identified by Erlanger (1990) are similar to what has been seen in GSE groups: relieving focus on present problems by affirming the individual as the recognized expert about him- or herself. The genogram becomes a visual representation of an individual's life story in which the present can be seen within the context of a lifetime.

Equipment list: A packet for each participant containing two blank genogram forms, family relationship form, key to genogram symbols, and sample complete genograms (it's best to print the genogram form on 11-inch × 17-inch paper for easy reading). Black ink pens. A lap board or tabletop for writing. Write-on board with boldly colored marker for the leader. Transparency projector with write-on markers or digital image project with computer input to display the genogram format.

Reminiscence: Decades of Life

Goals: It helps to gain a broad overview of life events and assign meaning to each decade.

Process: The leader introduces this approach to looking at life events within a 10-year context. Group members use one page for each decade of their lives to record personal information that is recalled from general discussion. Younger decades may be combined with a single group session given for decades beyond middle age. A more detailed review results from a single session for each decade. The leader sparks each discussion with questions about the people, places, things, and events that were important during a stated decade. Members are asked to reflect on this information between sessions and be prepared to give a name or description for that period at the next group. When this project is complete, members will have a review of their life in segments and will have assigned meaning to each decade. Some titles used by members in previous groups to describe decades are 0–10, most cherished time; 21–30, becoming independent; 41–50, rediscovering our marriage; and 61–70, decade of loneliness. Encourage members to draw a scene, house, person, object, or anything that represents the decade description. This drawing is the introduction to the information sheets. Leaders assist members in compiling all sheets into a memory notebook.

Outcomes: Using the broader time segment of 10 years makes it easier for group members to recall significant events within a range. Unlike other types of life review that search for good and bad events of the past, this project focuses on the happy, productive, and satisfying events of each decade. With prompting and within the group discussion, each member will find something worth recalling at various ages. This project affirms the individual's connection to others over the life span.

Equipment list: Packet for each participant containing separate pages for each 10-year span (0–10, 11–20, 21–30, etc.); blank page for drawing with each decade printed at top, and scratch paper. Markers or bold ink pens.

Reminiscence: Life Investment

Goals: Allow each member to reflect on how they "spent" their life to date and where they choose to "invest" future years.

Process: The leader introduces the concept of "investing" as the means of placing what is valuable to us in a way that gains a future return. Using a marker board and a marker, brainstorm with members for what *investing* and *return on investment* means to them in monetary terms. Then compare those terms with what they mean in personal terms with the day, creativity, and energy of their lives. In the second session, members are given a poster board with 10 columns. The last 2 are labeled *Today* and *My Future*. Members are asked to use scratch paper to create headings for the 8 other columns and discuss these as a group. Typical headings for life investment include spouse, children, grandchildren, work, church, sports, hobbies, military service, or community service. In the third session, each person much choose the headings for 8 columns that represent those places where she or he invested most of his or his life. The fourth session talks about how much each investment costs in terms of time, sacrifice, effort, and love. Using $100 in play money to represent a totality of life investment, members place amounts that signify their level of investment in each category. The only rule is that some part of the investment must be "saved" for the Today and My Future headings. This activity may require two or three sessions. In the final session, invite members to share what they learned about their own life investment and whether, on reflection, there was a good return or inadequate return in their life or the lives of others. Discuss ways in which each person can invest in the future of self and others in the group, family, or retirement community.

Outcomes: The investment concept is another tangible way to show how much of a person's life has been spent on self and others. This can lead to validation or more unfinished business and regrets. As previously mentioned, the depth of the negative emotional processing depends on the skill of the leader.

Equipment list: Play money from a toy store (or make play money using colored copier paper). An envelope for each participant. Small poster board with 10 columns drawn. Scratch paper. Marker board and boldly colored marker for leader.

Bibliotherapy

French Renaissance essayist Michel de Montaigne confessed that his life was the background for his essays, just as many works are influenced by the authors' lives. These personal reflections and stories resonate with the experiences of readers. The healing potential of the written word may have first been recognized by the ancient Thebans, who believed in the power of reading as a change agent. Centuries later, therapists borrowed the same idea, called it bibliotherapy, and used written communication to probe thoughts, feelings, sensory perceptions, and abstract concepts for therapeutic purposes.

Popular press book publishers, newspaper advice columns, and personal experience articles continue to gain acceptance in the consumer market as a kind of nondirected, do-it-yourself bibliotherapy. Self-help books are among the most popular means of dealing with life crises. The implementation of self-help in reading and following a program for behavioral change either alone or with a group has been useful in treatment of some psychological problems, notably alcoholism and anxiety (Mains & Scogin, 2003). Structured bibliotherapy requires more consideration in matching the individual's issues with meaningful, therapeutic reading. Bibliotherapy used as an element of the GSE group modalities is a therapist-facilitated process with literary works chosen to enhance, challenge, or support the individual's work within the group.

Bibliotherapy is an exceptionally flexible modality that can be adjusted for high-to-low-functioning groups as well as for persons with visual and hearing impairments. Use of this technique with geriatric groups is stylistically different than its traditional, more independent form. At one end of the spectrum is the pure self-help, self-selection that relies on comprehension, awareness of need to change, and implementation of change. The opposite end of that spectrum is highly directive, reader-assisted processing of information done with a therapist in individual or group work. The GSE groups, like many aging group programs, use a bibliotherapy approach that gives participants as much independence as possible, yet enough assistance to maximize enjoyment and prevent frustration. As Floyd (2003) cautions, the advantages of bibliotherapy can be negated for individuals with cognitive impairments or low attention spans. For that reason, the group leader becomes the reader for some groups or provides an audio book for repeated listening. Thus, structured bibliotherapy designed for the capabilities of each elder group is the context in which this modality is presented.

Reading about the emotions and difficult experiences of others provides a safe distance for processing feelings within an elder group. The candor that accompanies analysis of a fictional character's problems supersedes individual fears, guilt, or shame that sometimes inhibits ownership of problems (McKinley, 1977). This potential to recognize problems and solutions more easily when applied to fictional characters (rather than to self) is another reason that bibliotherapy is a useful treatment supplement for reducing depressive symptoms in elders with mild to moderate depression (Scogin, Hamblin, & Beutler, 1987). The magic of literature also allows readers to live vicariously through the author in experiences like hanging gliding, traveling across Europe, playing a piano solo at Carnegie Hall, or dancing the night away. The limitations of mobility, dexterity, or finances cannot restrict the pleasures of armchair exploration through literature.

Stages of Bibliotherapy

Four distinct stages occur in geriatric group bibliotherapy: receive, perceive, believe, and weave. First, the group members must be able to receive the material in either written or oral form. GSE prefers to use short written works such as essays, summaries, excerpts, or poetry. It is important to know the cognitive and reading skills of all participants. Retyping the material in large-print letters is appreciated by the group. For lower functioning groups, read brief segments with a pause to recapture attention. By knowing the group members' reading skills, the leader can determine how to present the material so that all can receive it.

Higher functioning groups may delve deeply into the characters, situation, resolution, and alternatives as well as identify with a character. Lower functioning groups deal with the surface issues and basics of the story or feelings expressed by characters. Keep in mind that bibliotherapy can be useful at whatever level the group operates. Even cognitively impaired groups, including Alzheimer's patients, can profit from bibliotherapy with therapist-directed discussion (Hynes & Wendl, 1990). Third, participants need to believe in the significance, usefulness, emotional catharsis, or some message worth receiving that is derived from the literature. Concurrently, they must believe that they can apply the message in a personal way. Finally, there is the ability to weave what is learned or felt into the participant's self-concept.

In traditional bibliotherapy, in which the participant is solely responsible for keeping up with reading assignments and making oral or written reports, there is no provision for physical and mental impairments. Because these conditions are increasingly prevalent with aging adults, adjustments must be made for greater inclusion. Here are some suggestions that have proven effective in GSE groups.

1. For visually impaired elders, retype material in 24- or 36-point type, make an audio recording of the material, or request a volunteer to read the material to the participant before group.
2. For hearing-impaired elders, place the participant close to the leader's right or left, whichever is the side of strongest hearing; check the participant's hearing aid for low batteries or other tuning; or print cue cards with key characters or discussion points to help the participant remain focused during the discussion.
3. For cognitively impaired elders, use brief, simple readings with fewer characters, read slowly, pause when group members disconnect and help them focus their attention, and select literature with distinct characters and easy words.
4. For slow readers and nonreaders, avoid distinguishing them from the remainder of the group. If you give printed pages to others, also offer them to these participants, make an audio recording of the material, or request a volunteer to read the material to the participant before group.

As you will see from the items used in the GSE groups, almost any reading material, poem, essay, or prose can become the focal point of a structured bibliotherapy. A mixture of classics, contemporary, and historical works are generally appealing to elders. Depending on the group's interests, they may be willing to try current or less familiar works.

Remember your best ally in preparing bibliotherapy is a librarian! She or he is trained to match literature with the reading interests and levels of all ages. A university research librarian can provide background on the bibliotherapy concept and related journal articles. However, it's the librarian at the local public library who can keep your group well supplied with suitable material and suggest new acquisitions. Take time to talk with the local librarian to explain what is needed for the elder groups. You may also discover such treasures as the bookmobile or a local poetry reading group that will visit your group on the librarian's recommendation.

Bibliotherapy Groups

Bibliotherapy: Enjoying Essays

Goals: Look at the simple things in new ways.

Process: The leader selects short (one- to two-page) essays that highlight commonplace life experiences. A wealth of material is available in popular magazines such as *Reader's Digest* and *Guideposts* and the back pages of several women's magazines. Give each group member a copy to read before the next group or to follow along during the discussion. If possible, retype the essay using large-size type for easier reading. Recruit a volunteer from within the group to serve as the reader for visually impaired members. During the discussion, the leader uses a large marker board to track comments. Begin by asking each member what this essay communicated to them. Next, look at the style and the tone of the writing. Finally, ask if anyone in the group relates to the writer's feelings or opinions. However, a lower functioning group can also enjoy shorter (one-page) essays and talk about basic meanings.

Outcomes: Essays are regaining popularity by calling attention to simple things that are easily overlooked in a high-tech, excessively complex world. Elder groups who are so removed from the fast pace of today's society relate well to these glimpses of a slower, more peaceful time in their lives.

Equipment list: Copies of articles or essays from magazines, newspapers, or bound collections at the library. Marker board and boldly colored marker for leader.

Bibliotherapy: What's New in Our City (State or Nation)?

Goals: Keeping up with current events.

Process: A high-functioning group is encouraged to propose and agree on several themes that will be pursued during upcoming groups. The leader verifies that each member has access to newspapers or magazines at the facility or brings in a folder with precut articles. For example, if the group theme this month is to look at issues that face the city, then all articles discussed will relate to people or events occurring in the city. Each member is asked to report on an article or broadcast news report. The leader writes each major topic on the marker board. After each person gives a brief verbal report, the group may decide which issue to discuss further during the session. The leader may challenge the members to write their own letters to the editor or to send a group letter. To further bring the outside world inside, invite local newsmakers or news reporters to talk with the group. This opportunity to be in touch with people who influence the news is very stimulating to this type of higher functioning group.

Outcomes: This activity restores a sense of connectedness between the elder and the world outside present boundaries.

Equipment list: Clippings from local newspapers and news magazines. Marker board and boldly colored markers for leader.

Bibliotherapy: What's Old Is New Again

Goals: Linking the past with the present through social changes.

Process: A personal sense of aging is not numerically bound; rather, it's tied to the first time we say "That's not the way we used to do it." Many elders retreat into the mistaken belief that they are totally unconnected with today's society. This bibliotherapy activity demonstrates the recycling of social trends that continually link past and present. Using popular literature, the leaders share a "new" idea, such as the emphasis on family values, working at home to care for small children, or living simply. Group members discuss each topic and recall any related experiences. The leader may also bring in older writings that predicted the future such as George Orwell's *1984* or Jules Verne's *From the Earth to the Moon* and *Twenty Thousand Leagues Under the Sea*. When reading excerpts from such works, talk about how close these predictions came to reality. Invite group members to propose other topics showing how old ways are being revived as new.

Outcomes: Members gain a wider perspective by seeing themselves as a part of a larger, fluid society with which they are not as out of touch as they may feel.

Equipment list: Newspaper or magazine articles about change and trends. A video or documentary about social trends. Library books.

Bibliotherapy: Myths and Fables

Goals: Examine how beliefs, superstitions, and legends emerged from ancient folk tales.

Process: The leader suggest several general topics such as Greek mythology, Aesop's fables, Homer's *Odyssey*, *Analects of Confucius*, or Hans Christian Andersen fairy tales and stories. The group selects a topic to read and discuss for two to four weeks. Excerpts are read aloud, with copies available to all members who desire to read the full work. The leader prepares large-type lists of questions for discussion. The group can be subdivided into teams or pairs to prepare comments on an assigned or chosen question. The initial discussions deal with the story, characters, setting, and moral of the story. Some groups may want to dig deeper by probing for feelings about the situation, story resolution, and comparable circumstances that individuals have faced.

Outcomes: This is a rediscovery of favorite stories or a new look at the origin of beliefs, superstitions, and legends that were accepted knowing the source.

Equipment list: Library books. Pictorial history books that show people and places in the time period of the reading material.

Bibliotherapy: Forget TV Shopping, Get My Catalog!

Goals: This is a nostalgic view of dreams and wishes from the past.

Process: The leader introduces the topic by asking members to recall the best (and worst) items they purchased by mail order. Talk about the thrill of discovery in the advertisement, the anticipation of awaiting delivery, and the satisfaction or dissatisfaction with the item ordered. Sharing these stories will bring out a range of feelings from humor to frustration. At the next group, display copies of old catalogs or catalog replicas. Let each member select two favorite items to share with the group. Read aloud the descriptions. Compare the quality, prices, and features of the old catalog items to similar newer items. Typically, you will find that several members recall ordering certain items and can discuss the experience in detail. At the next session, bring weekend newspaper ads for similar items at department and hardware stores. Look at the differences in items and advertising descriptions. Talk about how malls are intended to replace main street storefronts and whether group members agree with that objective. As a summary group, tune into a TV shopping channel to see and hear how items are sold in this video catalog approach. Discuss how the armchair shopping convenience of catalogs yielded to malls and is back again with TV shopping.

Outcomes: Using the common experiences of shopping, delve into the changing methods of acquisition and how the newest trend resembles the old method. This activity is fun and a springboard for reminiscence with high and low functioning groups.

Equipment list: Replicas of catalogs and advertisements from several time periods after the 1900s. Weekend newspaper ads.

Bibliotherapy: Attitudes about Aging

Goals: Expand perspectives on aging and seek positive input.

Process: The leader presents a text (book, collection of essays, or short stories) as a basis for discussion. Taking brief segments of a book or a single essay or short story, read aloud with members following along on copies. Effective material covers a variety of aspects of aging: health, loss, mobility, adult children, grandchildren, friends, retirement, money, changes in activities, worry, change, and expectations. Discuss the situation and the writer's viewpoint. Does the group agree or offer alternative coping strategies? How can such a situation be turned into a positive? What advice would the group offer? In brainstorming such questions to benefit a third party, group members can tackle difficult issues that are too sensitive to personalize.

Outcomes: Talking about aging issues at this distance gives more freedom of expression to test ideas before claiming them for oneself.

Equipment list: Book with poems, essays, or short stories. One favorite of GSE groups is *Old Is Older Than Me* by Maxine Dowd Jensen.

Bibliotherapy: Rhyme Me a Rhyme

Goals: Find meaning and expression in poetry.

Process: With high-functioning groups, the leader involves members in selecting a type of poem, specific poet, or period of poetry to read and study. Newly formed groups and lower functioning ones benefit from the leader selecting well-known works such as Walt Whitman's *Leaves of Grass* or Edgar Allan Poe's "The Raven." After reading the poem aloud, discuss its feelings, images, and mood. For groups who genuinely enjoy poetry, introduce some different styles of verse for other cultures such as Spanish coplas (couplets), the Rubaiyat of Omar Khayyam, or Rabindranath Tagore's "Fireflies."

Outcomes: Poetry is another means of reaching feelings and becomes a focal point for expressing them.

Equipment list: Books of poetry.

Bibliotherapy: Armchair Exploring

Goals: Launch an adventure that transcends physical boundaries.

Process: The leader gives each member an invitation rolled up as a scroll with a map and treasure symbols. Inside is a brief description of the journey that the group will follow with literature, pictures, and maps. Select a vivid and varied experience such as Homer's *Odyssey* or Marco Polo's travels. Discuss the planned route and show the area on a globe or map. If possible, pin up a map so that reading progress can be marked at each session. Divide the literary work into segments for reading aloud. Provide copies as requested. Discuss each episode, the critical event, the result, and what was learned by overcoming that obstacle. Encourage members to project themselves to that time and place as if they were members of the fictional exploration team.

Outcomes: This stimulates the imagination and creative thinking while providing a healthy escape from present circumstances.

Equipment list: Books, globe, map. Historical books with pictures of people, costumes, and places help set the mood.

Bibliotherapy: Childhood Rhymes

Goals: Examine the words, meanings, and historical roots of familiar nursery rhymes.

Process: The leader gives members a copy of a familiar nursery rhyme (or distributes different rhymes to each member). Well-known rhymes to read and discuss are "Mary, Mary Quite Contrary," "Humpty Dumpty," "London Bridge," "Little Jack Horner," "Ring Around the Rosie," "Little Miss Muffet," and "Twinkle, Twinkle, Little Star." After reading each rhyme aloud, discuss its meaning. Is this a rhyme to entertain or teach a principle to children? Does anyone know the historical background of the rhyme? The leader makes discussion notes on the marker board. Where information exists on the history and political overtones of a rhyme, share these with the group. Some rhymes were disguised as social and political comments applicable to their times. For example, "Mary, Mary Quite Contrary" is about more than a garden growing. Are there members of any present royal families whose behavior is quite contrary? Is there a political figure who is poised for a great fall, like Humpty Dumpty? Or is this metaphor applicable to the fall of the Soviet Union, split into too many parts to put together again? Write down the results of the group's creative thinking.

Outcomes: Here is another way to look deeper into seemingly simple words. Rhymes are reminiscent of childhood and parenting years. Higher functioning groups can complete the full range of this activity. Lower functioning groups relate to these rhymes and discussion about how they are part of childhood.

Equipment list: Books of children's rhymes and their meanings, with copies for the group. Look in the library for reproductions of early classics, such as *Mother Goose's Rhymes* (1760/1980). Marker board and boldly colored markers for the leader.

Bibliotherapy: The Crossroads of Our Lives

Goals: Reflect on the major choices and circumstances that altered the direction of life and recognize long-held beliefs about those crossroads experiences.

Process: The leader or group members read aloud Robert Frost's poem "The Road Not Taken." With this classic metaphor for life crisis, begin by asking each group member to share how one choice affected his or her life for the better and another for the worse. Give each person full attention in a kinder version of the Gestalt "hot-seat" method wherein the leader and group members ask questions with the intent of identifying each individual's strengths. The leader lists strengths that the individual and group hear in reviewing the personal story and transcribes a list of those strengths to give to each person. If this group takes additional sessions, begin each time by reading Frost's poem to set the mood. This activity may become more psychotherapeutic and therefore more appropriate for psychotherapists or psychologists as leaders. If facilitated by other health professionals or used with lower functioning groups, read the poem and steer discussion to the positive choices and good decisions of life rather than the traumatic events.

Outcomes: This exercise is a type of life review with poetry as basis. It can become very intense or remain limited to surface emotions, depending on the group's willingness to participate. At any level, this exercise airs and gives structure to the tendency to ruminate over roads taken and chances missed.

Equipment list: "The Road Not Taken," a poem by Robert Frost. Write-on board and markers for the leader.

Therapeutic Writing

"It's better to write about things you feel than about things you know about." L.P. Hartley's *The Process of Writing* has always been an emotional journey for the writer. As part of that emotional expression, writers learn about themselves. Writing can be cathartic and frustrating or uplifting and comforting. The groundbreaking studies of Dr. James Pennebaker demonstrated that something as basic as journaling has therapeutic value regardless of the skill of the writer. The Pennebaker Paradigm, a structured journaling process, was initially designed to help individuals cope with recent or past traumatic events (Pennebaker & Beall, 1986). Writing became an additional way beyond traditional talk therapy to express and come to terms with intense feelings.

Over the years of research, Dr. Pennebaker expanded the usefulness of journaling to a variety of contexts. His studies demonstrate the application of journaling for stressed college students, pain management, coping with chronic illness, and older adults forced into early retirement by corporate downsizing (Pennebaker, 1997). Whether or not the life situation was resolved, individuals with various emotional issues found measurable "health benefits" from telling their stories in writing (Peterkin & Perryman, 2009; Pennebaker, 2000; Pennebaker & Seagal, 1999).

While writing is personal and may be kept private in a journal, the act of journaling can be done in group. Kathleen Adams (2000) developed a workbook approach to writing for health and affirmed the value of using this process in a group. Since geriatric groups are geared to focusing on positive emotions and personal strengths from past experiences, journal writing can also be targeted toward positive. As Burton and King (2004) found, there are pro-health advantages to writing about "intensely positive experiences." This is consistent with the geriatric group goals to use a type of journaling as another approach that is closely associated with reminiscence and life review. Where journaling goes a step beyond those approaches is that the subject of the writing is the elder's feelings; beliefs; and, at least subtly, self-image.

The use of writing in geriatric groups needs to be adapted to match the cognitive abilities and writing skills of the participants. A group of community elders may be better able to find deep meanings in the journal and actually write in it. Some may have typing or computer skills and choose to journal in that manner. Elders in long term care who may be cognitively aware but have difficulty with holding a pen due to arthritis or other impairment need to have assistance in recording their words or use shorter exercises that require less actual writing. Another technique that is used with oral history and life review is to make a sound recording of the elder's journal entries. The recording can later be typed and given to the elder to look over. That recording plus the typed words are treasures that a group member may choose to share with family or keep private. The group leader has to access these factors before launching a journaling modality so that all group members can participate, and none are frustrated by the modality.

Journal purists may think that the GSE approach is "journal lite" with the adaptations. However, capturing the elder's thoughts in writing or recording as part of a structured journal modality has value for each participant in honoring their words and thoughts.

Therapeutic Writing Groups

Therapeutic Writing: My Life in Three Acts

Goals: Members reflect on their lives as a three-act play: early years, young and middle adulthood, and older adult years. In journals, the members write a story from these three periods that has a common or repeated theme.

Process: The leader introduces this topic by reminding the group that a play may be divided into three acts; for example, *Our Town*, a play by American writer Thornton Wilder in the late 1930s. The leader may decide to read aloud this play or read only sections to give examples. Group members over age 70 may have studied this play in high school. (A Baby Boomer group may not be as familiar with this work.) An effective way to use this modality is in five parts: introduction of the process, act one, act two, act three, and summary.

Outcomes: Older adults can feel that they are no longer the same person as they once were because of infirmity or age, which can be a factor in depressed mood. With this writing exercise, they make the connections of past events or actions and discover continuity between the younger self and present self that defines aging.

Equipment list: Copy of Thornton Wilder's play, *Our Town*. If possible, show a video of this play. The 1940 black and white movie is available online. Later adaptations may also be found in video format. Journals or pages with prompts for each act.

Therapeutic Writing: Characters in My Story

Goals: Recall several people who were influential or significant in years past, people who in some way shaped the group member's character.

Process: The leader begins with a brainstorming session, asking group members to identify people who were influential or significant in their past. The leader starts with categories on a marker board or poster boards. These categories are organizational and also serve as prompts: Parents, Brothers/Sisters, Other Family, Spouse, Friends, Coworkers, Teachers, Spiritual Leaders, and Military Comrades. Members may suggest other categories. After gathering a variety of names, ask each member to choose two or three people who were the "lead characters" in their life stories. In their journals, give one page to each "lead character." Write about why that person was important and how their lives were changed for the better because that person was a "lead character" in their personal stories. Invite members to share their stories with the group.

Outcomes: Poet Alfred Lord Tennyson said, "I am a part of all that I have met." Group members reflect on the part that their lead characters played in their lives and the positive memories about those individuals.

Equipment list: Marker board or poster boards, markers, journals, or pretyped pages with prompts to assist members with less digital dexterity.

Therapeutic Writing: Exploring Positive Feelings

Goals: By focusing on the feelings that are desirable, group members give less attention to negative thoughts.

Process: Using sentence stems on preprinted pages, group members of various writing skills can participate with a short answer or a longer response. The leader introduces the four feelings: Joy, Peace, Gratitude, Hope, then distributes four corresponding sheets. Members are asked to choose two feeling sheets and respond to the prompts. When all are finished, the leader invites members to share with the group the feelings they chose and what they wrote.

Outcomes: Feelings shared are feelings validated. In group, there are individuals at a similar stage in life who can relate possibly better than family or staff with each other's feelings. In this sharing, members are also stating aloud what they want to attract into their lives. The leader encourages members to use their written ideas to ask others for what they need and want.

Equipment list: Board with key feelings illustrated by photo or graphic. Preprinted sheets and markers. Examples of sentence stem sheets are as follows. Leave paragraph size space to expand on each prompt. Add lines to guide writing. Feelings of choice can be added with this format:

Joy

Joy is _____
I have joy when _____
I share joy by _____

Peace

Peace is _____
I find peace in _____
I share peace by _____

Therapeutic Writing: Letter to Myself

Goal: In writing a letter to the private self, each member acknowledges personal worth, dreams, and desires.

Process: The leader begins with a discussion about how each person has a public self (seen, known by others) and a private self (known only to self or shared with select others). As older adults lose the deep connections from earlier adulthood (i.e., spouse, best friend, closest sibling) either due to distance or death, the private self is protected behind the public self. Ask members to think about their private self and how this aspect of personality differs from the public self (i.e., may be more vulnerable or fun seeking than the public self). Then invite each member to write a letter from his/her public self to the private self. This writing remains personal. After the writing, ask members to share, not what they wrote, but how they felt in reconnecting with the wants and needs of the private self. Is there anyone in the present situation who could be trusted to know the private self?

Outcome: Giving value to the private self provides acceptance for the whole person. The private self may have become ignored for the elder who attempts to be what others want or expect because they feel that the private self would not be valued.

Equipment list: Journals and peaceful instrumental music playing in the background during writing. Audio recording and player.

Therapeutic Writing: Feelings into Form

Goal: Feelings can be difficult to describe and their impact varied by each individual's perception. Linking feelings to things that are visual provides a metaphor for understanding.

Process: The leader shows a series of vivid photos depicting concepts to be used in this writing exercise. Group members are asked to think of a recent strong feeling. Note: If the group leader is a professional, this exercise can be done first with negative feeling then with positive feeling. The processing for negative feelings requires a leader who can manage the situation and help members through negative emotions. If the group leader is not trained in psychotherapy, then guide members to choose a positive feeling. Show each poster that corresponds to the preprinted prompts on the worksheets. As the leader displays each picture/graphic, read the prompt, and ask members to write a word or sentence/s to explain the feelings connection. When finished, encourage members to share aloud their responses.

Outcome: In giving these feelings a tangible comparison, older adults may be able to better communicate their feelings to others.

Equipment list: Preprinted sheets, markers, and pictures/graphics. Here are some examples:

(Show color wheel) The color of my strongest feeling is _____

(Show four seasons graphic) My strongest feeling is like the season of

_____

(Show flowers, plants) My strongest feeling smells like _____

(Show weather thermometer) The temperature of my strongest feeling is

_____

(Show music or orchestra) Set to music, my strongest feeling sounds like

_____

Therapeutic Writing: Gratitude List: Then and Now

[Developed with Lynn Ellyn Robinson, MSCP]

Goals: For participants to acquire a clear view of the here and now and to distinguish positive attributes from past experiences to bring forward to present situations.

Process: The leader opens a discussion about gratitude by sharing examples of things for which he or she is grateful. As the discussion stimulates members to reflect, the leader invites participants to share aloud if they choose, then to list in their journals (or on a printed sheet of paper with lines for each item) at least three things for which they were grateful from early in their lives through adulthood. After the members finish their lists, the leader asks the group to list a minimum of three things in their present lives for which they are grateful. After a pause for reflection, the leader encourages members to share with the group what was surprising, enlightening, or similar on the two gratitude lists. If in a community group with more participants, the leader could divide the participants into small groups for this discussion.

Outcomes: Participants find strengths or positive memories that transform present negativity or apathy toward a positive feeling about self and others. By sharing aloud or in small group, participants enjoy a meaningful social interaction.

Equipment list: Marker board or chart paper and appropriate markers. Markers or other writing instruments, lined paper, or individual journals.

Therapeutic Writing: Positive Memories and Early Skills Recognition

Developed by Lynn Ellyn Robinson, MSCP.

Goals: For participants to acquire perspective relative to positive experiences and skill acquisition in their past and to experience heightened self-esteem.

Process: The leader will give examples of pleasant memories that group participants will be likely to have experienced. Examples include a time when they acquired or mastered a new skill; when they met someone or made a friend of someone who became significant in their lives (not necessarily a spouse); and an "aha" moment of discovery, such as when they distinguished something for themselves or had their first exposure to beautiful art or music, read a wonderful book, or got in touch with the beauty of nature. Each participant will be asked to describe a significant positive memory. The group leader then asks each participant to describe in what way that memory had a far-reaching positive outgrowth. Examples could include a meeting that turned into a close friendship, the trip to an art museum that set someone on the path of becoming an artist or appreciating art, or the deep-rooted love of nature that turned into ongoing activities intended to protect an endangered habitat or joining an outdoor group that provided wildlife adventures. Representations of significant memories would first be listed by the participant, or an appointed scribe, then drawn or collaged on craft paper or a poster.

Outcomes: Participants will re-experience the pleasure of discovery and distinguish the far-reaching connections with those positive events. While working at tables, small groups have the opportunity for reminiscence and fellowship.

Equipment list: Marker board or chart paper and appropriate markers, magazines (from which to glean pictures), brightly colored markers and/or colored pencils, plain or colored craft paper on which to draw or mount pictures, scissors, adhesives (glue sticks and/or tape).

7

GROUP MODALITIES
FOR THE BODY

For meaning is not in the event, but in the motion through event.

Robert Penn Warren

From birth, the physical body begins to age. Although that decline continues throughout the life span, a preteen is not called an aging child. Even adults escape the label of aging until reaching the culturally defined "middle age," which is marked by tacky party signs making fun of the 40th or 50th birthday as being "over the hill." What actually prompts feelings of aging is encountering disease, injury, or chronic pain, which can occur at any age.

Dr. August Weismann's Wear and Tear Theory (1882) warned that with years of poor maintenance and dietary abuse, the body would break down faster at the cellular level. In the normal aging process, the body's ability to repair damage decreases, so the more "wear and tear" on the body over the years means a significant impact in older ages. The amount of wear and tear on the human body may shorten that life span or dramatically reduce the quality of life and mobility. Today's older adults who are ages 70–80–90 lived during times when there were few conveniences at home or work. Early decades of their lives were spent in farming, heavy lifting in factory work, or the daily labors of pumping water, hand washing clothes, and attending to typical household chores. They continue to feel the impact from wear and tear from childhood to early adult years.

With aging and physical limitations come fewer opportunities for sensory stimulation and exercise as caregivers seek to make the environment safe. This loss of tactile contact combined with declining sensory perceptions creates a bland world. The sensory pleasures of sight, sound, smell, taste, and touch diminish in aging adults more as a result of apathy than of lack of ability. Inherent in the protection and safety issues of residential senior housing is the reduction of opportunities to engage the senses. Meals are prepared in a restricted-access kitchen and served without the elders' having the enjoyment of smelling the food as it cooks. That's just one of many ways elders in residential care become removed from common sensory experiences and dependence on sensory perception.

Another problem is one of physics: A body at rest stays at rest while a body in motion can continue movement. Older adults with mobility limitations are quickly ushered to a chair or secured in a wheelchair for their safety. While that is a concern, what about the value of allowing the body to move as much as possible? Something as simple as chair aerobics or swaying arms to the music heightens the older adult's sense of awareness and body connection. Another approach to encouraging movement among elders is to introduce the ancient art of Tai Chi. When properly adapted for the abilities of the group, Tai Chi offers new options for helping elders improve balance and experience heightened sensory awareness in a group activity (Li, Harmer, Fisher, & McAuley 2004; Voukelatos, Cumming, Lord, & Rissel, 2007).

Reconnecting to the Sensory Environment

Restoring whatever degree of sensory enjoyment is possible for the elder group is yet another comforting connection with the familiar, enjoyable experiences of the past. The key to communicating with elders who have cognitive or speech impairments can be through sensory awareness with the alternative of nonverbal responses. Even early memories have sensory detail that helps the individual relate to time and place that amplify the experience (Kabat-Zinn, 2005). The multisensory experiences that prompt delight and wonder in children become, in later years, the awareness and themes an older adult finds from those memories and that can become a part of positive coping (Clark, 2008). Bryant (1991) found that creative approaches to the sensory awareness group makes therapy viable for persons who cannot otherwise participate effectively in verbal, task-oriented groups. McMurray (1989) noted that painting and clay modeling used in art therapy have the added bonus of appealing to several senses: tactile, smell, and sight.

Sensory perception comes from the five senses: sight, smell, touch, hearing, and taste. Sensory stimulation activities for geriatric groups generally incorporate four domains: visual, auditory, tactile, and kinesthetic. With advanced age, eyesight (visual) and hearing (auditory) may be supported by assistive devices (eyeglasses, magnifying glass, hearing aid). Depending on the physical condition or chronic pain problems, movement (kinesthetic) and locomotion can be limited. For many older adults the sense of touch (tactile) remains even if actually holding or manipulating objects is hampered by arthritis or other dexterity problems. Kabat-Zinn (2005) affirms the basic need for human touch does not diminish with age. Color awareness and word associations with colors are often rooted in early memories, and these color impressions are significant to reaching these early memories (Clark, 2004).

Some tactile activities may also have the sense of smell, such as a examining a bouquet of varied flowers with different textures and scents. Taste is more difficult to add into the modalities because of the dietary restrictions that group members may have. Generally speaking, assisted care facilities forbid bringing in foods or drinks for the group. While this limits the use of taste for sensory stimulation, it does not eliminate the possibilities. Work cooperatively with the facility staff to find taste options that are appropriate to the dietary needs of group members. Don't assume that this is easier when working with community elders who can make their own choices. The choices made might be counterproductive to diet or allergies and cause a new problem. Unfortunately, for these reasons, there are few safe options to incorporate taste for sensory awareness. Understanding the sensory domains is important in planning group modalities designed for sensory stimulation.

GSE groups encourage the use of senses to the fullest extent possible for each participant. No assumptions are made on the basis of physical limitations. For example, an elder with severe arthritis may not be able to hold a velvet scarf and discern the texture with her hands. With the elder's permission, the group leader can rest the velvet scarf on her arm or gently let the fabric touch her cheek where there may be greater sensory awareness. If tactile sensation or vision is limited, approach the senses with vivid word pictures. The touch of silk communicates softness, so find the words for that feeling. Using descriptions such as "like baby's skin, a feather pillow, or fluffy cotton balls" also gives the impression of being soft without touching an object.

Borrow Ideas from Children

Another way to expand sensory awareness activities is to watch children around the home. What unexpected things bring squeals of delight? Soap bubbles, digging in the garden, and making doll-sized pies from dough scrapes. These are sensory experiences—sometimes whole body experiences such as rolling in the mud or sliding down a rope.

Ask teachers trained in early childhood education to share ideas they use for sensory awareness. No one needs to teach children the Gestalt concept of the "here and now"; that's the world they occupy in sensory exploration. Sensory-oriented activities can help older adults connect with the "here and now" as a positive distraction from worry, pain, or sadness. Children gravitate toward sensory activities, adults ignore them, and elders are restricted from them. Sensory experiences are small pleasures to be enjoyed by all ages, not just by children.

Body/Sensory Groups

Body/Sensory: Back to Nature

Goals: The feel of soil, beauty of flowers, and satisfaction of being involved in something that is alive and thriving.

Process: Choose a spring or fall time that is suitable for conducting this group outside. Set up on a picnic table or card tables for all members. Distribute supplies to members' "workstations" before they arrive. After each member is seated, offer a choice of two plants to repot. Open group with a review of the steps for this project. State each step simply. Prepare a one-page instruction sheet of the steps for high-functioning persons. If this is a low-functioning group, take each step slowly and wait until everyone finishes before beginning the next step. While working, either (a) initiate a discussion of prior gardening experiences, or (b) go around to each person and ask them to describe his or her experiences. The leader makes certain that each plant is labeled. On one side of a small, flat stick (such as a tongue depressor or ice pop stick), write the plant's name and on the other side write the member's name. Depending on the preferences of the facility, growing plants may not be permitted in the patients' rooms. The leader can place all plants in a larger box and tend them outside. These growing plants can be brought back in a few weeks to admire, enjoy, touch, and discuss the pleasure of being part of their growing process.

Outcomes: The first time GSE used this activity, the results were amazing. Even the most sullen, withdrawn man in group became as animated as a laser light show. He dug joyfully in the dirt, finished his plants, and then spontaneously offered to help other members. When asked how he felt doing this activity, he responded, "I'm touching the good earth where life is. Do you know they never let us get dirty around here?" This activity is another example of how the cleanliness necessary for an assisted living home means some loss of simple pleasures like digging around flowers. Over the years, most of our group members had either lived at some time on a farm or visited relatives on farms. Planting, gardening, and working with nature are familiar and comforting for many elders. This activity is a springboard for reminiscences with some groups; for others it is a nonverbal, very sensual experience.

Equipment list: Small bedding plants purchased four–six per grouping. Potting soil. Plastic scoops or spoons. Small clay pots or recycled margarine tubs. Popsicle sticks or physician's tongue depressors. Enough supplies for each participant to have two completed plantings. One-page instruction sheet.

Body/Sensory: Baking Party

Goals: Re-create the sights, sensations, smells, and enjoyment of baking bread.

Process: This takes prior coordination from the facility or careful planning if used with nonresidential community groups. Each member begins by cleaning his or her hands and getting seated at workstations. With larger tables, seat three–four people per table. They form a group within the group for discussion while the project is underway. Let each person grease a small pan, knead the dough, and form a loaf in the pan. Write names of initials on each pan. As these return to the kitchen to rise and bake, clean up the work areas. The leader initiates a discussion about this activity or lets the group move toward reminiscence of bread baking at other times. As members share feelings or memories, the leader prompts for more sensory information. The next day or at the next group, return the completed bread to be admired and eaten.

Outcomes: Smells, sounds, sights, and tastes of home baking are frequently associated with significant times (childhood, first home) and special people (mother, wife, friend). All of these senses are recaptured in this activity along with potential for reminiscence and fellowship at the work tables.

Equipment list: The facility dietary kitchen prepares bread dough ready for kneading. Small disposable bread pans or cupcake tins. Tables covered for use in kneading the bread. Several plastic containers.

Body/Sensory: A Bit of Florida Sunshine

Goals: Enjoy the color, smell, feel, and taste of peeling and eating oranges.

Process: Here's a simple activity that combines several sensory elements in sharing conversation while peeling and eating fresh oranges. As group members are peeling the oranges, the leader asks each person to take time to smell and touch the fruit and asks each to try to find something new about it that he or she has never noticed before. Florida orange growers say their crop comes from the sunshine tree. Engage the group in a discussion about what brings "sunshine" into their lives or recall memories of picking and eating fruit fresh from the source. If weather permits, conduct group outside or save this activity for a cold winter day when changing the focus to a sunshine theme may reduce those seasonal doldrums. Confirm with the facility staff or individuals in community group that members can taste oranges without any dietary or allergy problems. If uncertain, limit activity to the touch and smell of the oranges.

Outcomes: The use of various senses is rivaled by the sheer pleasure of the activity. Some members with arthritis or other digital impairments may need assistance getting started. The leader needs to prompt members to help each other and enjoy the fellowship. This is a messy yet tactile experience that is suitable for all group levels (subject to dietary approval).

Equipment list: Fresh oranges. Plastic, rimmed plates or bowls. Lots of napkins.

Body/Sensory: Solve the Mystery without Looking

Goals: Stimulate connections between thinking and touch or smell to identify an object.

Process: Before group, the leader prepares a collection of items that may be identified by touch or smell. Higher-functioning groups may enjoy making a game of this by pairing members or dividing into teams. Cheer on each team as they use their sensory perception to solve the most mystery items. Here are some items that are effective in this exercise. In small canisters, saturate cotton balls with peppermint oil, rose oil, lemon, vanilla extract, or perfume; or use a small piece of strong lime. In separate paper bags, place a hairy kiwi fruit, pine cone, sponge, bar of soap, small potato, and lettuce leaf. As each person is trying to name the mystery item by smell or feel, prompt him or her to describe the items. This sensory activity can prompt a game-like atmosphere with lots of laughter and fun. Note: For lower-functioning groups, go around the room with items on a tray and let each person select one mystery item. Engage the attention of the others as each person tries to describe the mystery item with the leader's assistance.

Outcomes: Exploring common items in a nonvisual way stimulates the senses to support the process. This is particularly enjoyed by persons with impaired eyesight who are not receiving ample opportunities to motivate their other senses.

Equipment list: Clean, recycled black plastic film canisters. Paper bags. Fresh fruits and other mystery items.

Body/Sensory: We're Forever Blowing Bubbles

Goals: Sensory experiences with touch and sight.

Process: Gather the group outside. The leader begins by blowing bubbles. It's the rare elder group in which someone won't break into song about "forever blowing bubbles." If you can find a recording, play it or lead the group in singing a cappella. Then give bubble bottles to each member and invite them to join. Direct their attention to the form, size, and rainbow colors that appear in the light. The leader takes a cue from the group's comments for a discussion of bubbles as either metaphors for personal dreams and wishes or fun memories of blowing bubbles with their children.

Outcomes: This carefree activity is a pleasant break between more serious topics in a multisession program or as an introductory session with a new group.

Equipment list: Small bubble containers are inexpensive in multipacks at some toy stores. Audio recording of bouncy, lighthearted instrumental music.

Body/Sensory: The Sensation of Color

Goals: Associating colors with sights, sounds, smells, and touch.

Process: The elder generation was raised on the nonvisual imagery of classic radio programs. In a similar manner, this sensory exercise seeks to stimulate images or tell a story using other senses. Work with one primary color at a time to focus concentration. For example, the leader begins by talking about the color red. Give each member a piece of red paper or red fabric as a reference during this activity. Point out other reds in the room. Ask each member to tell one thing that reminds them of red. Then play a tape or make "red" sounds such as a fire siren (red truck, red in fire), a bold trumpet note (red as brassy), or tires screeching (putting on brakes). Show red objects (red pepper, beach ball, toy, fire truck, etc.). Inquire if anyone associates red with any strong smells, tastes, or touches.

Talk about how each person feels when surrounded by the color red. The leader can read short items from color psychology literature or decorating books on the types of persons attracted to red. Continue as long as the group is involved, before proceeding to explore another color and repeat the exploration. Colors stimulate vivid images and feelings for at least some group members.

Outcomes: The full range of senses is probed in relation to colors. Eyesight is not critical to this activity. As long as the person has experienced colors, he or she can participate well. One of GSE's oldest group members who had long ago lost her eyesight as a result of illness greatly enjoyed "the colors thing." Her imagination and enthusiasm for relating feelings to colors was extraordinary.

Equipment list: Audio recording of sound effects (look in library or request assistance from a local radio station). Any other sound-producing items (e.g., toys, bells, household items). Sound-book toys have wonderful audio images. Box of primary color crayons, colored paper, or colored fabric.

Body/Sensory: Fantastic Fur and Feathers—Pet Visits

Goals: Combines touch with enjoyment and memories of animals.

Process: Several days before group, be certain that no member is afraid of or allergic to the animals that will visit. If so, offer that member the choice to remain outside group or join another activity. For an in-depth study of pets as therapy, review the literature. GSE's most successful pet activities involved visits from a large, gentle dog that later came to live at the facility. A GSE therapist brought several sizes of parrots and, the favorite, an elegant blue macaw. These birds were tame and under her direction would perch on the arm or chair of group members. The conversation flowed easily when pets visited the group.

Outcomes: Caring for pets brings back memories of childhood and families. The feel of patting a live animal who returns enthusiasm gives a small, yet meaningful feeling of care giving that elders so often miss.

Equipment list: Calm, people-loving pets such as larger dogs, large birds, rabbits, and hamsters.

Body/Sensory: Seashore Sensations

Goals: Various elements common to the seashore are used to distinguish textures.

Process: The leader sets the mood with a verse or short reading about going to the seashore. Prompt members to identify common seashore items that are mentioned within the introduction (reread slowly if needed). Then invite members to touch and identify these items from the tub displays. Create a tub with a built-up sandy beach area, small shells, and water reaching the beach. One or two other tubs are all sand with shells buried so that each member can find several shells. Then take the shells to a washing area. In the background, play instrumental music with seashore sounds. Encourage members to talk about past experiences at the beach.

Outcomes: The sand, water, and shells are typical of the seashore and easy to bring inside for an armchair visit. The differing textures, shapes, and activities often keep a group so involved that they are reluctant to leave. Integrating the sounds of the sea with audio recordings enriches the experience.

Equipment list: Marker board. Several large buckets or plastic washtubs for creating mini-seashore and beach areas. Shells (purchased or well cleaned if natural). Sand. Small scoops. Cleanup supplies. Audio recordings of instrumental music with seashore sounds. Short reading or verse about the seashore.

Body/Sensory: Smooth or Rough

Goals: Group members identify familiar objects that are smooth or coarse, then discuss how each is used.

Process: The leader gives each member a different object to hold and examine during the introduction. Going around the group, the leader asks each person if his or her object is smooth or rough. The leader and the group ask questions about the characteristics of each object that suggest whether it is smooth or rough. After everyone has a turn, the leader takes an object, describes its texture, and talks about phrases that give sensory information. Some commonly used sensory-oriented phrases are "rough as a cob," "going against the grain," "smooth as silk," and "slick as glass."

Outcomes: Distinguishing textures is suitable for all functioning groups. Some elders are highly sensitive to rough textures (even scratchy clothing labels), so be alert that the rough objects are handled carefully. Textures are often keys to reminiscences.

Equipment list: Collection of objects that are smooth (satin, velvet, feathers, soft fur) and coarse (sandpaper, corduroy, bark, pine cone).

Music and Movement

> Music produces a kind of pleasure which human nature cannot do without.
>
> Confucius, *The Book of Rites* (ca. 500 B.C.)

From the sounds of the first primitive instrument to those of a keyboard synthesizer, music styles change, but music itself never goes out of style. A familiar example of the therapeutic aspect of music is found throughout the Psalms in the Bible. David perfected his performance skills playing a lyre or harp to the sheep as a shepherd boy. Later, in composing the lyrics that we know as the Psalms, the boy who became a king expressed intense emotions of joy, pleasure, fear, and depression in his music. For David, music was a calming influence, a mood enhancer, and a reflection of life. He may have been one of the first music therapists.

The tone, tempo, instruments, and arrangement of music are combined to evoke certain mental and physical responses from the listener. Funeral music isn't played to a rock and roll beat. "Happy Birthday" isn't sung like the blues. The emotional content of the music is underscored by its sound. In addition, there is a physical response to music: toe tapping, hand clapping, or moving with the beat. The crisp notes of marching music correspond with the patterned steps. A waltz or lullaby elicits a smooth, gentle, floating movement. Research by Phillips-Silver (2009) affirmed a lifelong connection that demonstrates "music and movement is pervasive in human experience."

In planning music as a group modality, pay attention to the elements of the music along with the expected mental and physical responses. Music makes connections with the senses and memories in ways that words fail, particularly for cognitively impaired or highly anxious patients. Soft, easy-paced music, including contemporary instrumentals and light classics, are an excellent background for beginning a group of restless and agitated patients. Instrumental music with nature sounds as background also provides a calming influence. Hanser (1988) reviewed various studies that demonstrated the power of music to reduce psychological and physiological reactions to stress. Nursing studies have demonstrated the value of music to reduce depressive symptoms (Siedliecki & Good, 2006) and calm agitated patients with dementia who do not respond well to verbal calming efforts (Goodyear & Abraham, 1994; Hicks-Moore, 2005).

In the same way that depressed or anxious patients can join their feelings in bibliotherapy with those of fictional characters, music can be used to focus, process, and express deep feelings. Elder groups need not avoid plaintive, blues-type music. Rather, it is to be used with proper preparation and processing within the group.

Value of Music in Elder Groups

Music creates an affective, pleasurable response and stimulates a cognitive response. The nature of these responses is linked to the listener's mental abilities. Higher-functioning groups generally enjoy an approach to music and movement that is a mixture of affective and cognitive processing. Lower-functioning groups are more comfortable working with one process at a time, predominately affective and reminiscence. Regardless of cognitive levels, music as a modality has six primary functions in elder groups:

1. Listening: The obvious advantage is personal enjoyment for the listener. In addition, music attracts nonverbal and shy persons into the group.
2. Discussion: Impressions of music are individual and neither right nor wrong. Sharing opinions about music and its message is a nonthreatening topic. Using music that is highly identified with life stages, the group has experienced results in many spin-offs for discussion from the music and lyrics.

3. Identification: Group members can relate well to music both by the mood and by the lyrical message. For example, a person who diminishes his or her own feelings hears a melancholy song and realizes that this is a more valid representation of his or her emotional condition than a false smile.

4. Reminiscence: Music is associated with many significant life events. There is the song claimed by a dating couple as "our song" and remembered for generations. Elders remain tuned to the pop music of their young adult years (Frank Sinatra, Irving Berlin, and big band singers for the middle- and oldest-old; rock and roll will be added as the generational music of Baby Boomers). Music is an effective modality alone or in support of reminiscence, spirituality, sensory stimulation, recreational therapy, art, and other modalities.

5. Sensation: As a sensory experience, music is satisfying to the musician and to the listener. The musician is not the only one with a hands-on option. Listeners get into the act with hand clapping, foot tapping, head bobbing, finger snapping, and shoulders swaying. Sitting close to an orchestra is the best way to feel the sound vibrations. However, using relaxation techniques, groups can simulate the experience of a live concert by visualizing the sights, sounds, and energy of the recorded music.

6. Action: Experiencing the sensations is part of the action in music appreciation. Whatever the physical capabilities of the elder group, a simple movement exercise can be designed to make the most of a natural inclination to move with the music.

Group leaders need to consult with the treatment team or physician to determine the suitability of the movement exercises for each group member. A separate approval and release form that explains the activity may be signed by the elder or the elder's guardian, trustee, or health care surrogate. Smart leaders also consult with an exercise physiologist or recreational therapist for suggestions on incorporating movement for various levels of physical and cognitive conditions.

Whether using the simple hand or head movements for physically limited persons or full body motion, the concept of music and movement as a combined therapeutic modality is used increasingly for elders as well as persons of other ages. Some types of regular exercise leads to psychosocial and physiological improvement for elders (Burlew, Jones, & Emerson, 1991). Music shared is a nonthreatening way to build rapport among the group. As Murrock and Higgins (2009) noted, "another way music alters mood is by encouraging social interaction." Hearing a song that is commonly known to the group is likely to have members begin to share memories of dancing to that song, singing in a group, or recalling memories associated with that song. In this way, music is part of the group identity.

The movement segments are usually short and interspersed with a resting period for listening or discussion. The purpose is not to work up a sweat but rather to gradually engage a range of motion, posture (standing and sitting), and passive stretching. The music is a hook to gain attention and participation. Elders tend to be resistant and full of excuses for avoiding exercise, as are many adults.

Emphasizing the music and socialization aspects of this group overcomes much of that resistance. The leader constantly reassures group members by working with realistic goals, verifying the suitability of activity to each member, arranging a comfortable environment, and giving opportunities for in-group socialization as well as acknowledging efforts (Burlew et al., 1991; Ferrucci & Simonsick, 2006).

Disagreement exists among therapists on whether to segregate wheelchair patients from or integrate them with ambulatory patients. Burnside and Schmidt (1994) advocated for separation, whereas the GSE program prefers to keep members within their regular groups regardless of physical limitations. GSE leaders feel that to remove and isolate wheelchair members is emotional discrimination and a threat to group cohesiveness. When necessary during the activity, the leader gives alternate movements for those who are physically limited—the same way responsible aerobics instructors show both high-impact and low-impact alternatives to their spandex-clad classes. More agile members or volunteers can become the partners of wheelchair patients, helping with arm movements, or gently guiding lifeless feet in tapping to the music. Working together so that everyone participates at some level is an important element in developing group cohesion and appreciation for each other. The caring and touch given one elder by another can be the most therapeutic aspect of this or any group modality.

Music and Movement Groups

Music and Movement: Big Band

Goals: Swing music gets feet tapping and arms moving for physical and mood enhancement.

Process: As the group enters, play a peppy big band song to set the tone. Members are seated in straight-back chairs with space between for arm movement. This is also suitable for wheelchair patients with some assistance. The leader introduces the songs, then suggests and displays simple movements with the music. Arm circles, head nodding, hand clapping, simulated drumming, feet tapping, rocking the body side to side, and stepping forward and then back are gentle moves that many ambulatory persons can perform to music. Assist patients in wheelchairs or with limited mobility by offering to carefully guide arms or feet in time to the music. If possible, invite the facility's physical therapist or community recreation leader for elder activities to direct the movements.

Outcomes: Moving to familiar music is pleasurable and provides some exercise.
Equipment list: Audio recording of big band music. Chairs.

Music and Movement: World War II Music

Goals: Music and memories of a place, time, and significant event are linked. In this global war effort, music was an important coping mechanism that can be an encouragement in present difficulties.

Process: The leader brings an anthology of World War II music on audio recording or on sheet music if a piano or portable keyboard is available. If possible, arrange the music in chronological order. Play a song, and then ask members to recall when they first heard the song, what was happening in their lives, and how meaningful this song was in coping with their emotions during that time. Invite musically talented members to play the melodies while the group joins in singing or humming. With higher-functioning groups, give copies of the lyrics to encourage singing along. Caution: This music will not have significance to Baby Boomers and some of the young-old.

Outcomes: These musical memories track the nation's response to war and victory in a period that personally affected elders and their loved ones. Identify the music and the messages that gave them strength and how they still use coping skills.

Equipment list: Recordings, sheet music, and books of World War II songs. Audio recording or keyboard.

Music and Movement: Marching

Goals: Parade tunes and military marches are background music for movement activity.

Process: Play a crisp parade march as group members enter. The leader reads a brief comment about parades or shows photos of major parades such as Fourth of July parades or the Thanksgiving Day Parade in New York City. Talk briefly about memories of watching or participating in parades. Spend at least half the session doing marching movements to well-known music. The leader acts as drum major, directing the group to march in place, wave, swing arms, and march around the room to music. Wheelchair patients join the parade with an assistant pushing the chair. Choose music that is energetic enough to get feet tapping without overexertion.

Outcomes: Invigorating for body and mind. The parade-movement connection is a natural for encouraging participation among physically able persons.

Equipment list: Recordings, sheet music, and books of parade and march music. Piano or keyboard. Drums and homemade cymbals.

Music and Movement: Patriotic

Goals: Involve several senses through stirring patriotic songs.

Process: A slower patriotic song plays as members gather. Members take their seats in chairs arranged with movement space between. The leader displays the flag and invites members to rise or, if in a wheelchair, show attention and join in singing the national anthem. If there are group members from other nations, make an effort to get a recording of their national anthem as well. After returning to seats, members are given kazoos or cymbals as their instruments to play in time with the music. Play a song and prompt members to play their instruments and sing if they choose. As a break between songs, let members comment on personal meanings they ascribe to the patriotic music. This activity can be done as part of a music series or saved for patriotic holidays.

Outcomes: Hearing, singing, humming, and hands-on instruments offer several methods of sensory involvement in this music and movement activity. Even lower-functioning groups participate well in this exercise.

Equipment list: Recordings, sheet music, and books of patriotic music. Piano or keyboard. Kazoos or homemade cymbals for each participant. U.S. flag.

Music and Movement: Nature Sounds

Goals: Relating musical imagery with sights and sounds of nature.

Process: The leader introduces the exercise as a way to see with the ears and imagine being in a forest or on a beach through the music. If the leader is trained with guided imagery, the experience becomes even richer for participants. With imagery, this musical nature exploration also becomes a relaxation exercise. If not used with guided imagery, play part of the recording while everyone listens. Then replay the recording, and ask for members to speak out and identify a nature sound. Encourage members to describe the image they get from listening to the music. After discussing the nature sounds on the recording, play a final time.

Outcomes: Through this type of music, a group with limited mobility can travel in their imaginations to places out of their reach. Memories of travel and childhood experiences emerge. Lower-functioning groups respond very well to this exercise.

Equipment list: Audio recording of music with nature sounds such as rain, waves, wind, birds, or storms.

Music and Movement: Sing-Along Songs

Goals: Recapture the enjoyment of a family activity popular before television, singing around the piano.

Process: Before the group's arrival, arrange chairs in a semicircle around the piano. At each chair, place pages with lyrics typed in large print. The leader and a volunteer serve as director and musician. Warm up with a few easy songs. Invite members to share a memory about family or neighborhood sing-alongs. Continue with songs, varying the tempo and ending with upbeat, positive songs.

Outcomes: Re-creating a pleasurable time and singing familiar tunes is a comforting, nostalgic activity.

Equipment list: Audio recording, piano, or keyboard. Copies of song lyrics in large type.

Music and Movement: Trip to Hawaii

Goals: Music from the tropics encourages fluid movements and senses of the exotic.

Process: Surround the group room with colorful streamers, artificial flowers, and tropical posters. The leader or guest instructor explains the activity of enjoying Hawaiian music while performing a chair-side hula. Each person gets a paper lei and two streamers. Using a video as a guide or copying movements from a book on hula, the leader demonstrates some basic movements, while waving the streamers. If you don't know actual hula hand movements, make them up as you go. Play a song, and give suggestions for movements. As the group gets more involved, play a hula song with lyrics, and instruct them to use any movement desired to communicate the message. Anyone who prefers to may stand and sway carefully with the music. Patients in wheelchairs and those less steady on their feet remain seated. With lower-functioning groups, the leader can get them moving, then go around to each person and encourage or guide them to move with the music. If the facility will allow, serve punch and finger-food-sized tropical fruit bites to complete the island experience.

Outcomes: Tropical music motivates listeners to move and sway easily in keeping with the rhythm. Group members will also recall many of the Hawaiian songs as part of their musical memories.

Equipment list: Audio recording of Hawaiian music, both instrumental and vocal. Optional video of dancers performing hula. Colorful paper leis and artificial orchids. Borrow tropical posters from a travel agent. Streamers of crepe paper or ribbon approximately one yard each (two per person). Bite-sized pieces of tropical fruit if not prevented by dietary restrictions.

Music and Movement: Outdoor Concert

Goals: Simulate an outdoor concert with recorded music in a comfortable outdoor setting.

Process: Before group, the leader arranges for sturdy outdoor chairs to be placed on the facility patio or adjacent yard. Clear a safe walking and wheelchair path. Bring a portable audio recording player with speakers. If possible, bring coffee or lemonade and snack foods to enjoy during the concert. When the group is seated, the leader introduces the music and tells something about it. Good choices for the activity are Broadway show tunes or light classical music. Another wonderful option is to have a local high school musical ensemble perform a live concert.

Outcomes: Enjoying music outdoors is reminiscent of town square bands performing on summer afternoons. A casual atmosphere and fresh air enhance music appreciation for groups of all function levels.

Equipment list: Audio recording with speakers adequate to be heard outdoors. Coffee or lemonade and snack foods appropriate to group.

Music and Movement: Hand Bell Chorus

Goals: Another participatory adventure in music with easy movements

Process: The leader may borrow hand bell sets from a local church or band. These bell sets may be heavy and not as easy to handle for group members with less grip or arm strength. If not available, any kind of bells will do. The least expensive method is to use small holiday decorator bells joined by a ribbon chain. The sound is not nearly as important as the participation. With higher-functioning groups using actual hand bell sets, the leader can point to the person as a sign to ring the bell. Otherwise with this group or low-functioning groups, ring or shake the bells in time to the music.

Outcomes: The sounds may vary, yet making music as a group is a satisfying activity for many elders.

Equipment list: Hand bell sets or homemade bell chains. Audio recording for background music.

Music and Movement: Tai Chi and Harp

Developed with Cynthia Burnley Trower.

Goals: The gentle sound of harp music is easy listening and associated with angelic images that bring comfort and a positive distraction from physical, emotional, or spiritual distress. Harp music brings comfort and relaxation to people who suffer physically, mentally, emotionally, and spiritually. When adding Tai Chi, the two elements combine for body awareness that promotes a mind and spirit connection.

Process: Tai Chi is an ancient Chinese art practiced by persons of various ages, including older adults. This activity is done in coordination with harp music. Unless the group leader is trained in Tai Chi, bring in a guest leader who is a trained Tai Chi master and understands how to adapt movements for older adults. The harp music begins to set the mood, then the leader or guest leader helps each group member to find a position that is an arms-length space from the next person. The guest leader demonstrates deep breathing and each movement for the group. The movements are fluid and graceful, many of which can be performed by persons from a chair if standing is difficult. Group members need to be able to follow basic directions to join the activity. Older adults with multiple physical impairments or balance problems are not suited for this activity. Request physician or facility approval for participation of all group members.

Outcomes: The blending of Tai Chi movement and harp music has the potential to reduce stress and give sense of mastery over body and mind.

Equipment list: Audio recording and player with adequate speakers. Harp music in continuous play for the length of the activity. Recommend that group members wear pants and shirt suitable for movement with flexible shoes.

Music and Movement: Tai Chi and Water Music

Developed with Cynthia Burnley Trower.

Goals: Blending the movements of Tai Chi with nature sounds connects with group members on two levels: physical and sensory. While following the movements, the sounds free the mind so that even for elders in long term care, there is a sense of taking a mental vacation away from cares of the present day to a peaceful refuge.

Process: The Tai Chi leader (guest leader or group leader with Tai Chi training) coordinates the movements with the changes in the nature sounds. For example, at the sound of water fowl flying, the group is asked to "move your arms like wings, like a crane taking flight."

Outcomes: Participants will feel as if they experienced the nature area, and their bodies will be refreshed by gentle movements and deep breathing. Without exercise equipment, Dr. Yeh of Harvard Medical School says the Tai Chi arm exercise may "strengthen your upper body . . . [and] core muscles" (Harvard Health Publications, 2009). Older adults with multiple physical impairments or balance problems are not suited for this activity. Request physician or facility approval for participation of all group members.

Equipment list: Audio recording and player with adequate speakers. Harp music in continuous play for the length of the activity. Recommend that group members wear pants and shirt suitable for movement with flexible shoes.

Remotivation

> Skill to do comes of doing.

> Ralph Waldo Emerson

Remotivation groups seek to restore an incentive for greater participation in the activities of daily living and, if possible, creative pursuits. The technique was developed for psychiatric patients from the ideas of Dorothy Smith, who worked as a hospital volunteer in the mid-1950s. She used a five-step process to engage withdrawn and socially isolated patients based on her belief that regardless of the impairment, some aspects of the core personality remained. The concept attracted the attention of Smith, Kline & French Laboratories, which funded a 1956 project to develop a manual for remotivation groups in hospitals and long term care facilities (Robinson, n.d.; Sullivan, Bird, Aplay, & Cha, 2001). In 1971, The National Remotivation Therapy Organization was formed to develop professional training for this process for groups, which is defined as "designed to help clients by promoting self-esteem, awareness and socialization" (NRTO Policy & Procedure Manual, 1995, p. 3). The National Remotivation Therapy Organization provides classes, seminars, and web access training for therapists as well as family members who want to apply remotivation techniques.

In developing the basic handbook on remotivation, Bierma (1998) emphasized that the technique focused on what the client/patient provided as beneficial merely for the participation without criticism of the content. In conducting remotivation, the group leader does not lecture or judge, uses third-person questions to elicit information in a nonthreatening manner, and makes certain the conversation is appropriate to the verbal and cognitive abilities of group members (Bierma, 1998). Over years of clinical application, remotivation has grown beyond a behavioral foundation to include affective elements. Observing elders' progress in remotivation is like peeling an onion. The outer layers are tough and seem unconnected to the core. Further into the layers is a concrete level of thinking that distances self and others from emotionality. Near the core are feelings, memories, and values that are suppressed until the individual discovers reasons to be involved in the present and care about the future. Part of shedding the layers of ambivalence involves reminiscence, sensory awareness, and socialization within the group. Considering this process, remotivation is both distinct and interdisciplinary, making it difficult to categorize. In the GSE approach, remotivation is part of modalities for the body because of the emphasis on connecting the whole self with a place or topic presented in the here and now. Even when reminiscence is included, remotivation targets positive outcomes for the person in the present time.

From a functional perspective, remotivation is sometimes linked with reality orientation. Clearly, there are differences in purpose and theory. Reality orientation is used with confused elders and psychiatric patients who are disoriented as to person, place, and time. Reality orientation is definitely different than reality therapy. The latter was developed by Glasser (1965) to foster social responsibility and self-reliance in delinquent adolescents. Folsom (1968) is credited with developing reality orientation for rehabilitation of geropsychiatric hospital patients. Key components were based on consistent repetition by all staff members of the patient's name, the day, the time, and place; and directions around the unit and on calmly yet firmly stating requests.

Blended Approach

GSE's approach to remotivation incorporates some of the elements of reality orientation into remotivation groups. This blended mix of remotivation and reality orientation spiced with reminiscence and sensory awareness is also used with varying degrees of effectiveness in other group programs (Hern & Weis, 1991).

The structured approach for remotivation groups is based on Dorothy Smith's five steps:

> 1. Climate of Acceptance, 2. Bridge to Reality, 3. Sharing the world in which we live, 4. Appreciation of Work World, 5. Climate of Acceptance. (Sullivan et al., 2001)

This format is adaptable for groups of all ages and many types of therapeutic issues. Applying these steps for older adult groups provides predictable structure, which creates a sense of comfort to older adults in knowing what to expect.

The GSE remotivation sessions are based on the same high level of acceptance and appreciation for each member, regardless of what the member communicates.

Equal value is given to members who are present but contribute less or not at all. Showing value to each individual is imperative for the group leader in developing rapport. Every GSE remotivation session begins with a simplified reality orientation wherein the leader greets every member by name and welcomes the group to this day (mentioned by day of week and date). The leader may also color a weather map from the newspaper (cold shown in blue, hot progressively in shades of yellow to orange) and asks something about the weather or the season.

Before beginning any activity, the leader explains briefly what activity is planned and precisely how members can participate. As a group becomes more cohesive, the leader may declare an open period of 5 or 10 minutes for anyone to make a positive statement to the group or to offer a general issue for discussion. With community groups who may have more connection to outside events via newspaper or broadcast media, be certain to set the ground rule that this is not the time to bring up political, religious, and/or social issues. A gentle redirection from the group leader in a way that is not judgmental is sufficient to move past topics that can become negative or intimidating. Lower-functioning groups need structure and respond to repeated reality orientation during the activity. Allowing open discussion time is counterproductive with cognitively impaired, confused, or wandering persons.

GSE groups progress through a series of stated topics to elicit individuals' responses and eventually to group interaction by alternating topics and activities. As with traditional remotivation, discussions and participatory exercises are geared toward a specific theme that may be as basic as performing an activity of daily living or more thought stimulating as family holiday traditions and travel experiences.

Adaptation to present circumstances and improvement in attitudes about self and others that lead to acceptance are ongoing goals. Secondary goals are defined by the needs of each individual in group. A rambling talker who monopolized conversation may find his or her energies redirected toward hands-on activities to focus energies on a task. The shy, suspicious newcomer who prefers to ignore others in favor of solitary activities is given a working partner or some type of encouragement to verbally interact with others. The leader gleans ideas for goals from the facility treatment team report, from family or physician recommendations, and by monitoring individuals within group. GSE has also used a variation on remotivation as an adjustment group for newcomers to a long term care facility. Remotivation groups provide an entry-level experience for determining the suitability of newcomers for other more active or affective groups.

Traditional remotivation groups meet for a stated period, such as 12 or 14 weeks, leading toward closure. GSE groups and other nursing home groups work with the same patients for a longer period of time or at additional times owing to losses in functioning, coping, or adaptation to new circumstances. Thus, GSE remotivation groups are more open ended, allowing members to flow in and out according to their progress and needs.

Leader's Role in Remotivation

The most effective remotivation leaders are focused, encouraging, and capable of conducting task-oriented groups. These highly structured activities also require more outside group effort in planning, organizing, and preparing materials. While conducting groups, the leader continually monitors and guides each member toward achievement of individual goals. Thus, remotivation groups place a large demand on the leader's skills and energies. A larger group (more than eight people) functions better with coleaders who share duties. Coleaders alternate presenting the activity and monitoring members' progress, or coleaders share presentation responsibilities yet divide the members for monitoring and redirection.

In addition to stated individual goals, remotivation leaders look for overall positive responses from group members, which include but are not limited to the following: (a) active listening, (b) verbalizing appropriately in discussions, (c) attentiveness to the activity, (d) ability to remain on task, (e) responding to reality cues, (f) accepting redirection, (g) making an effort to communicate with other group members, and (h) demonstrating or expressing positive feelings in group.

Effectiveness of remotivation and reality orientation are widely debated in the literature without consensus. GSE leaders working in long term care geriatric facilities agree with the findings of Murphy, Conley, and Hernandez (1994) that remotivation activities are simple to implement, promote interaction among members, and are rewarding experiences for the leaders. Overall, GSE remotivation groups with high- and low-functioning members have been a nurturing ground for positive change and renewal of social skills in the small-group environment.

Remotivation Groups

Remotivation: Meet and Greet

Goals: Giving attention to each individual and his or her interests helps the group begin to know each other.

Process: The leader welcomes each person on his or her arrival and assists in finding a seat or wheelchair space in the circle. When everyone is seated in the circle, the leader puts on a name tag and introduces him- or herself, then brings a name tag to each person, repeats his or her name, and asks the group to greet the person by name. Next, the leader tells a basic preference about him- or herself, such as "My favorite color is blue" and writes blue on the second line of the name tag. The leader goes around the group, repeating each person's name and asking about his or her favorite color. The member can write that information on the name tag, or the leader can offer to do so. Next, the leader repeats this process with a third piece of identifying information such as "My home state is Tennessee." As a way of incorporating the information and recognizing each person, the leader then turns to the person on his or her left and says "I want to introduce

Mary. Her favorite color is yellow and she is from Georgia." Next, it's back to the leader. When this exercise is repeated with the same participants, solicit different information to complete the second and third lines.

Outcomes: Acknowledging members by name and giving attention to any aspect of their uniqueness is uplifting for self-esteem and may diminish fears of being lost within a group.

Equipment list: Large-print name tags with two additional lines. Washable markers.

Remotivation: Day and Month

Goals: Orientation to time and place.

Process: The leader greets each person on arrival and gives a name tag with first name printed in large letters. After all members are seated in a circle, the leader goes around the room, stating each name and inviting the group to greet each person by name. In directing attention to the large calendar, the leader circles this day with a brightly colored marker. Group members are asked to look at this mark and tell anything they can about this day and month. The leader confirms or corrects this by stating that, for example, "This is Monday, February 5" and pointing to the date, then asking if anyone has a birthday today or in this month. The birthdays are marked on the calendar (and the leader keeps notes of upcoming birthdays). Are there any other important events in the month of February? What and when? What do people associate with Monday (back to school, first day of work week, blue Monday, etc.)? During the discussion, the leader makes several casual repetitions of the day and month and points to the calendar for visual reference.

Outcomes: Becoming aware of day and date is important in restoring a sense of relationship to the rest of the world, from which institutionalized and mobility limited elders feel disconnected.

Equipment list: Marker board. Large calendar for current month. Brightly colored markers. Name tags.

Remotivation: Weather and Season

Goals: Orientation to time and place by associating weather with season.

Process: The leader welcomes each person on arrival and gives him or her a name tag with first name printed in large letters. If there is a window in the group room, the leader directs everyone's attention toward it. If not, the leader describes weather conditions outside and asks the group what season this appears to be. How do they know? What are the signs, colors, and feelings of the season? The most effective visual used in GSE groups is a color weather map from the local newspaper; *USA Today* has this type of map if the local paper does not. The national weather map uses colors to designate temperature. Even low-functioning groups do well in relating blues with cool and reds with hot. The leader points on the map to the geographical location (city and state) of the group. What does the map say about this season? Can group members identify states where they previously lived and tell something about the weather there on the basis of the map colors? The leader then discusses any special events, holidays, or activities that are associated with this season.

Outcomes: Using the newspaper weather map as a focus, members get a bigger picture of what is happening seasonally around the country rather than just what is outside their windows. Talking about seasonal weather in different areas brings out discussion of contrasts: Snow may be falling in the Northeast while it is sunny in the Southern coastal states. Weather, both extreme and normal, is a trigger for reminiscence. Members relate to where they have enjoyed spending time during the present season or other seasons (i.e., winter in Florida or Arizona, Maine for summer, etc.). Weather may be associated with loneliness (snowbound winters), planting gardens (spring), going on vacation (summer), or returning to school (fall). Other reminiscences about surviving a hurricane, tornado, or ice storm can be turned from a negative to a positive by drawing out how the member overcame hardships and what was learned from the experience.

Equipment list: Color weather map from this day or previous day's newspaper. Name tags.

Remotivation: Current Events

Goals: Enhance orientation toward present time by focusing on current events in the world outside one's immediate view.

Process: The leader greets each person on arrival and gives him or her a name tag. After everyone arrives, the leader writes on the board the day, date, and year. Group members are invited to comment on anything that is special about this date. The leader then shows the newspaper with the headlines of several articles highlighted with marker. Members can volunteer to read the headlines, or they may choose to pass. After reading the headline of each story, the leader inquires if anyone knows more about the story. The leader can summarize or read excerpts from any story, then invite comments. He or she can balance the serious news items with a few human interest stories and avoid stories that hinge on violence and political or racial conflict. As each story is discussed, the leader asks group members if this story affects them and in what way. In repeating this group, the leader will discover that some groups are more interested in international news and others in local news. Think like a headline news service and try to cover a variety of different issues.

Outcomes: Few people of any age are without opinions about what is happening in their world. However, elders may appear as if they do not care about current events because their views are not sought. Keeping up with current issues encourages elders to think about problems and concerns outside themselves.

Equipment list: Local newspaper or current news magazine. Name tags. Marker board and markers.

Remotivation: Welcome New Member

Goals: This structured activity introduces a new member to the group.

Process: Like neighborhood organizations that provide a welcome basket to new residents, the group's welcome approach gives more than a passing "hello" to a new member. The leader introduces the new member by name and gives two facts about him/her that were learned before group started. Each member is asked to state his/her name and give a "gift" to the new member; the gift is something nontangible. For example, a member might say, "My name is Annie and I give you a smile when you need one," or "My name is Les and I will show you where to find places if you get lost." The leader or assistant can write a list of these "gifts" and the names of the givers to present to the new member after group.

Outcomes: By hearing the names and associating each with a "gift," the goal is for the new member to feel comfortable and connected to other members. Making the new member the center of attention in a positive way also demonstrates value.

Equipment list: For a group with adequate writing skills and digital dexterity, the leader could give a card and marker on which each member writes a "gift." Alternatively, the group leader writes the information on a note pad and later types it on an attractive page. Typing in a larger handwriting-style font will be easier for the receiver to read and enjoy as a keepsake.

Remotivation: Beach Ball Toss

Goals: Group members relate through an activity.

Process: The leader greets each member and gives out name tags. After a brief time of mutual greetings, the leader explains a game that involves recognition of others. The leader gives each person a colored ribbon to wear loosely around the neck. Try to alternate the colors in a clockwise format so that red ribbons are at positions 12:00, 3:00, 6:00, and 9:00; blue ribbons are at positions 1:00, 4:00, 7:00, and 10:00; and yellow ribbons are at positions 2:00, 5:00, and 11:00. Adjust for smaller numbers of participants. Play light instrumental music in the background. When the music begins, start passing one beach ball around the circle so everyone can handle it. This can be done standing or sitting; however, all participants need to be in the same position, either standing or sitting. The leader coordinates the ball toss by calling out the color. If the leader says "Pass to red," then the person with the ball can pass it to anyone who wears a red ribbon; if the leader says "Green, pass to green," the ball is passed from one person with a green ribbon to someone else wearing the same color. A second beach ball can be added if manageable without frustration. Limit to one beach ball for lower-functioning groups to reduce confusion and enhance concentration on the task. Divide the direction; first ask the member to point to another person wearing a red ribbon. After that is done, then ask the ball be passed to the identified person with the red ribbon. Higher-functioning groups or those with good arm mobility may enjoy a faster pace with two beach balls and more variety in calls. This game is active and keeps everyone involved. It's also a good break between more intense group activities or for a day when group members are fidgety or distracted.

Outcomes: Cooperating in a game that is easy for all to play is enjoyable and stimulates the cognitive-physical connections.

Equipment list: Several medium-sized, light beach balls in different primary colors. Instrumental music recording and player. Colored ribbon. Name tags.

Remotivation: Letter-to-Word Association

Goals: Making connections between letters and words stimulates thinking and memory.

Process: After greeting each member and giving him or her a name tag, the leader introduces a new activity with the excitement of a television game show. One approach is to give an alphabet block to each person. Going around the room, the leader asks each member to show the block, say the letter, and then give one word that begins with the letter. The leader can repeat the word or write it on the marker board. Going around the room, each person gives a word begin-ning with that letter. The process is repeated for all members. A faster moving variation is for the leader to pick a letter, write it boldly on the board, then ask for word associations. Another option is for the leader to select a letter, get a response, then let the respondent select the next letter, and so on. Applauding efforts and creating excitement add to the jovial atmosphere.

Outcomes: Sometimes the shy or reluctant members are more inclined to get involved in a game than in a discussion. It's easy for all levels. Even GSE's cogni-tively impaired groups participated enthusiastically in this activity with a slower pace and single-step directions.

Equipment list: Marker board. Optional: alphabet blocks with related pictures. Name tags.

Remotivation: Show and Tell

Goals: As members participate, they are encouraged to verbalize and also share the spotlight.

Process: The leader welcomes the group, distributes the name tags, and intro-duces the activity. Each person is given a paper bag containing one commonly used item. The leader demonstrates the show-and-tell process in three steps: first, by looking into the bag and recognizing the item; second, by showing the item to the group and telling what it is; and third, by talking about some ways this item can be used. After the presenter is finished, she or he asks if anyone knows more ways to use the item. The process continues until all members have a turn at show and tell. If, on looking at the item, the member has any confusion or dislike, he or she can ask for another item. In discussing the items, there will be both factual content and reminiscence. The group applauds each person's effort.

Outcomes: This simple activity allows each person to be the expert and receive positive attention from the group.

Equipment list: A collection of lightweight, easy-to-hold common items such as a spiral notebook, teacup, kitchen timer, tape measure, trinket box, small flashlight, and garden tool. Paper bags. Name tags.

Remotivation: Transportation

Goals: Group members recall methods of transportation they have used and related experience.

Process: After the welcome and mutual greetings, the leader displays a collection of photos or models that represent methods of transportation. If there are enough items, the leader gives one item or photo to each member. Taking turns, each member shows his or her item, names it, and talks about how it is used to transport people. After every member presents an item, the leader asks for names of unusual forms of transportation or those that have not been discussed and writes them on the board. These may include rapid transit subways, moving sidewalks in airports, elevators, escalators, ferry boats, and more exotic methods like the space shuttle, submarine, or hang glider. Discussion can evolve in several directions: reminiscence about favorite type of transportation in the past, a vehicle that was desired but never tried, or how popular means of transportation have changed during group members' lifetimes. The group may vote on their first, second, and third most popular transportation vehicles.

Outcomes: This topic is flexible and encompasses many common experiences. People of all levels of functioning seem to enjoy this discussion and tend toward remininiscences of first cars and interesting experiences in train or boat travel.

Equipment list: Pictures or models including cars, trains, trucks, buses, airplanes, helicopters, ships, and bicycles. Marker board and markers.

Remotivation: Rocks and Shells

Goals: Group members identify and relate objects from nature to their sources.

Process: Following the welcome and greeting, the leader invites members to participate in the armchair nature exploration that will compare objects from the seashore with those from the mountains. The leader displays rocks and shells of different sizes, shapes, and varieties. Preparing large-type cards with a brief description of each item before group allows the group members to assist in presenting the items. As each type of rock or shell is passed around for inspection, the leader asks members to comment on how it looks, feels, and smells. Does it remind them of any personal experience? Have they ever collected rocks or shells? What are some ways to use rocks and shells for decorating or jewelry?

Outcomes: This activity brings familiar objects from nature that have sensory and reminiscence potential. People at all levels of functioning enjoy handling and discussing experiences with finding or collecting rocks and shells.

Equipment list: Labeled samples of rocks, granite, quartz, and shells. Library books with background information and photos of different types of rocks and shells.

8

GROUP MODALITIES FOR SOCIAL SKILLS

We don't stop playing because we grow old. We grow old because we stop playing.

George Bernard Shaw

Among today's older adults, retirement was anticipated as the "golden years": a time to relax, play, socialize, and reap the benefits from decades of work. Many imagined spending happy days at senior adult communities or moving closer to adult children to enjoy grandparenting. Gradually that idyllic scene is interrupted by the death of a spouse, chronic illness, physical impairments, cognitive impairment, or a combination of factors that lead to social isolation.

Humans are social beings. Whether a life-of-the-party extravert or contemplative introvert, older adults retain their social interaction styles and preferences refined over many years of social choices. For those with a limited social circle of close family and a few friends, each loss pushes them further into a lonely existence. Others built their social circles around work and career, so after retirement those connections fade.

Regardless of age, social connectedness remains a significant aspect of life satisfaction. Older adults who maintain or expand their social circles tend to report better quality of life and are healthier than their age cohorts who lack a social network (Glass, deLeon, Marottolie, & Berkman, 1999). The stimulation of conversation and companionship seems to have therapeutic value that Mendes de Leon, Glass, and Berkman (2003) found to be a factor in delaying cognitive regression and injuries leading to disability among community dwelling elders.

Older adults face discrimination called ageism, an attitude that their grandparents and great-grandparents did not experience as widespread as it exists today.

Ageism is a type of discrimination based on age, broadly applied to persons who are older or who appear older. Of this stereotyping and exclusion, one of gerontology's pioneers, Dr. Robert Butler, was concerned that younger adults use ageism "to cease to identify with their elders as human beings" (Butler, 1975, p. 35). This devaluation of older adults further reduces their opportunities for socialization and involvement in activities and organizations where younger voices prevail.

In a brief yet stunning sentence, House (2001) defined the problem as "social isolation kills." How and why social relationships positively impact health and well-being is not adequately proven; however, epidemiological research has identified social isolation as a health risk (Brummett et al., 2001). As a basic antidote to social isolation, House (2001) recommends that connecting individuals to one or more others who could form a social circle could have a major health-affirming impact. Social engagement, whether within a small group or a large group of friends and family, provides encouragement and acceptance as demonstrated by Cohen-Mansfield et al.'s (2007) study of a large sample of Shared Interest Groups within a low-income senior housing program. Berkman et al. (2000) look at the benefits of "social influence" in "giving meaning to an individuals' life" as part of a group or community. Pasupathi and Carstensen (2003) agree that older adults need social interaction; however, they found that older adults place more value on "emotionally meaningful and rewarding interactions" than on a more random style of socializing. The emotional value of socialization is increasingly significant at older ages than what is seen among middle or younger adults.

In reviewing studies on social connection and pro-health behaviors, Berkman et al. (2000) concluded that regular participation in a social network is an important factor in sustaining self-efficacy for older adults. That is the concept of GSE geriatric groups in which the goals for these older adults are to strengthen their connection with others, do things together, and develop relationships. Regardless of the modality used, the therapeutic value of geriatric group work is in joining individuals for a common purpose. To address the social needs, GSE modalities engage humor, art, and photos. These are familiar aspects of their lives—familiar and inclined to prompt the discussion and sharing from which social interaction occurs.

Humor

> There are no things by which the troubles and difficulties of this life can be resisted better than with wit and humor.
>
> H.W. Beecher

Laughter is a medicine too often overlooked in geriatric treatment. Leaders and students who are new to geriatric work are inclined to make the mistaken assumption that humor is not appreciated in a nursing home or retirement community.

Such an assumption is another manifestation of therapeutic prejudice. If we applaud the efforts of entertainers and staff to bring laughter to terminally ill children and young adults in a cancer ward, why do we disregard the healing potential of humor for elderly persons? Clearly we are not laughing at the plight of age, illness, or immobility any more than we are laughing at the ravages of cancer. What we are doing is providing an alternative focus by encouraging elders to laugh with us. Norman Cousins's (1979) *Anatomy of an Illness as Perceived by the Patient* makes a strong case for humor even in dire situations on the basis of his use of laughter as part of his healing experience. Understanding this principle is the key to appreciating humor as a geriatric group modality.

GSE groups use a variety of techniques that connect to the humor sources of and memories from the elder's past. Transitioning to humor after more intense modalities helps both the leader and the group members avoid group burnout. The physical and emotional release of hearty laugher can be prompted by anecdotes from magazines, videos of children, jokes, or asking elders to recall their favorite funny stories from their families. Another method of therapeutic humor gaining popularity for use with older adults is Laughter Yoga, applying the physical and emotional release of laughing in a group without need of external jokes or prompts (Shahidi et al., 2011).

Efficacy of Humor

Humor studies are no laughing matter (pardon the pun). The Association for Applied and Therapeutic Humor (AATH) describes humor therapy as "any intervention that promotes health and wellness . . . a complementary treatment of illness to facilitate healing or coping, whether physical, emotional, cognitive, social or spiritual (AATH, 2000). Humor in group work functions as an anxiety regulator (Tuttman, 1991), strengthens the treatment alliance (Schnarch, 1990), and increases social interest (Rutherford, 1994). A year-long study (McGuire, Boyo, & James, 1992) on the effectiveness of humor with 86 nursing home residents substantiated the benefits of humor as an intervention for improving the perceived quality of life. Ewers, Jacobson, Powers, and McConney (1983) considered humor a necessary tonic for seniors in residential care. Their program used a variety of activities and resources in what they called the "humor toolbox." Joel Goodman's Humor Project (www.humorproject.com) teaches health care professionals how to guide patients in identifying the humor in everyday events and applying humor in their life situations. At Morton Plant Mease Hospital in Clearwater, Florida, GSE leaders learned some approaches from the Comedy Cart that includes a multimodal collection of resources brought directly to the patient or group. With a similar concept, the Elder Clowns and Laughter Bosses from the SMILE program evaluated humor therapy for 400 residents in long term care facilities with goals of improving life satisfaction, alleviating depressed mood, and promoting cooperative behaviors (Brodaty, Low, Chenoweth, & Fleming, 2011). The SMILE study showed a decrease in agitation among residents with dementia at rates comparable to antipsychotic medications, and the therapeutic effect remained after completion of the training program as continued by staff members (Australian Nursing Journal, 2011).

The leader who is comfortable with humor is likely to best use this modality. Without becoming a comedian or a performer, merely show yourself to the group as a person who enjoys a hearty laugh and desires to share that pleasure with others. Franzini (2001) endorsed the rapport building potential of humor as well as the need for more therapists to be trained in proper use of humor to support and not damage the client's self-efficacy. The most effective humor for geriatric groups is universal, appropriate, and respectful—not sarcastic or political. Some groups are more willing to personalize humor, and others prefer to keep it at a distance. Laughing together creates closeness and equality between the group leader and the group as it does between the therapist and client (Dimmer, Carroll, & Wyatt, 1990). Humor begets humor. Let laughter flow freely, and allow group members to rediscover how humor brings joy to the moment regardless of their present circumstances.

Humor Groups

Humor: Classic Radio Comedy

Goals: Return to those laughing days of yesteryear and enjoy them anew.

Process: The leader beings by asking group members to recall their favorite comedy on the radio. Who was the star, and what type of situations were typical? Because radio was such a significant family entertainment source, many elders have vivid memories of gathering in the evening to listen to regular programs. After a brief discussion, the leader plays a portion from an old radio show. Another way of using this material is to play short segments from several shows and make a contest of identifying the names of characters and shows. With low-functioning groups, use only short segments, and identify the characters.

Outcomes: Not a sound was wasted in creating word pictures for the radio comedy audience. Thus, these programs do things to the senses and the imagination in ways that television cannot duplicate. The involvement and entertainment are suitable for persons at all levels of functioning.

Equipment list: Audio recordings of old radio shows and player. Test volume to determine if extra speakers are needed in the group room.

Humor: Classic Television Comedy

Goals: Similar to radio comedy, this is for enjoyment with more visuals to support the humor.

Process: As with old radio shows, the leader asks the group to recall their favorite television comedies and characters. Display the videos of classic TV shows, and briefly talk about how easy it is to record and replay with today's technology. Ask members to share their first experiences with a television set and how it compared with the radio. Play a short introductory scene to be certain everyone can hear and see well. Make adjustments before beginning the video. Use a library video or record the shows, skipping commercials to reduce time and maintain the program's continuity. If time permits, discuss the most humorous scenes and what caused each person to laugh at this show or character.

Outcomes: Television best captures nonverbal humor with body motions and facial expressions. This is another means of provoking laughter and temporary escape into a less serious environment.

Equipment list: Video player, videos of classic TV comedy, and large-screen television.

Humor: Sharing Jokes

Goals: Exercise spontaneous humor.

Process: The leader can open group with a brief comment on the history of jokes or launch right into reading jokes. At any time, group members are welcome to interject a joke they recall. Appropriate limits may be set, such as no foul language and nothing that demeans a race, gender, religious, or ethnic group. A method to get others involved is to copy jokes in large print, with each joke on two cards—the opening part on one card and the punch line on the other. Color code the cards. After the blue-card reader gives the opening part, the other blue-card reader completes the joke.

Outcomes: Demonstrates how laugher is another kind of "medicine" for groups.

Equipment list: Joke books from bookstore or library. Clip and save jokes from *Reader's Digest* and other magazines. Color-coded cards with jokes in large print.

Humor: Mature Humor

Goals: Finding humor in aspects of aging.

Process: Introducing this topic, the leader shares a funny situation in which she or he was involved. This group gives space to laugh at personal frustrations by laughing with others. The leader shows a series of mature humor cartoons or reads jokes and a few brief stories. Members are encouraged to interject at any time their humorous experiences since moving to the facility (if residential) or in the past year (for community elders).

Outcomes: There are so many serious aspects to aging (pain, limited mobility, and memory loss) that the ability to laugh at ourselves and our frustrations is a positive coping strategy.

Equipment list: Book of jokes or essays with a humorous look at senior adult life. Cartoons or articles from senior magazines such as *AARP: The Magazine* or *Reader's Digest*. A GSE favorite is *A Treasury of Senior Humor* by James E. Myers.

Humor: Essays

Goals: Finding humor in the commonplace.

Process: The leader selects a series of humorous essays that deal with ordinary aspects of life. An alternative is to choose several essays from different authors on a single subject, such as waiting in the doctor's office or struggling with child-proof medicine bottle caps. Talk about what elements of the situation are funny and share any similar experiences. Does the author convey humor with unusual words, dialogue, or convoluted situations? With several essays on a single subject, discuss how each author used a different style to create humor.

Outcomes: Finding humor in everyday life reminds members of the many possibilities for laughter no matter what the circumstances are.

Equipment list: Library books of well-known humorists that the group will recognize such as Erma Bombeck, Dave Barry, or Andy Rooney. Essays found in magazines or newspapers.

Humor: Innocent Humor of Children

Goals: Re-experiencing humor through children's viewpoints.

Process: Presenting children's humor can be done with photos, video recordings, or reading. Even videos of the preschool play, a children's parade, or young children telling knock-knock jokes are ideas for this group. The leader can also read from a children's joke book. Many of those jokes seem timeless. You will be surprised at how many jokes have been passed down through several generations of children.

Outcomes: Enjoying laughing with children and recalling humor from childhood experiences.

Equipment list: Books on humorous things children say. A memory trigger for older adults is *Kids Say the Darndest Things* by Art Linkletter or the newer version by Bill Cosby. Video of children, video player, and large-screen television.

Humor: Jesters of Our Lives

Goals: Remembering the people who brought laughter to us.

Process: The leader shows a photo of the court jester and speaks about this character's role as a medieval comedian. Give group members a few moments to think of the person or persons who always knew how to bring laughter and levity to them. Who are the jesters they have known? What was special about those persons? What was their style of humor? Can they recall their favorite jokes or comic actions?

Outcomes: Learning to recall the people from our lives who shared humor with us.

Equipment list: Photo and article on court jesters.

Humor: Clowns

Goals: From childhood through adulthood, clowns symbolize fun that is ageless.

Process: The leader surrounds the room with clown photos and bright balloons for a party atmosphere. If possible, invite several local clowns to assist with group. Begin by introducing the visiting clowns or showing videos of clowns. Set up a face-painting station for any group members who want to participate. Start a discussion about their first experience with clowns and how they appear through a child's eyes. Allow the clowns to present a skit or engage members in a simple activity. Bring a digital camera and offer to take a photo of each member with the clown.

Outcomes: This activity is pure fun and offers a chance to feel like a kid at the circus again.

Equipment list: Photos or videos of clowns. Invite a local clown troop to visit. Add balloons and face-painting station. Individual and group photos to give to each as a keepsake.

Humor: Comics

Goals: On the comic page are laughs about all ages and stages of life, with something that appeals to everyone.

Process: The leader brings enough Sunday comics for every member. With volunteers from the group, take turns reading the comics aloud. Talk about some of the long-lasting comic strips. What makes their characters transcend several generations and remain funny? What are some older comics that are no longer printed? Would those characters and situations still be funny today?

Outcomes: The comics are good for laughs and reminiscences about how humor has changed over the years.

Equipment list: Sunday comic pages (in color). Classic comic books.

Humor: Family Funnies

Goals: This is a retrospective on family life and humorous events that are part of the family legend.

Process: The leader begins with a personal story or brief essay about a funny family situation. The group is invited to share those special stories about relatives or events that become the legends of laughter in each family.

Outcomes: Family humor is deeply personal and satisfying to recall.

Equipment list: None.

Expressive Art

Art belongs with life itself.

Max Eastman

Art and expression are inseparable twins of human emotions that appeal to all ages. Every culture and society produces art that reflects its lifestyle, values, and experiences. Elders in group programs have seen a number of different artistic styles representative of social, cultural, and political changes during their 60-plus years of life. During their lifetimes, art became both varied and plentiful. How often is critical notice given by a passerby to the poster reprints at the discount stores, the original unheralded landscapes at craft fairs, or the painted-on-velvet portrait of a dog or deceased rock star hawked from the street corner vendor? Although not exactly in the same category as the original masterpieces displayed at the local museum or university exposition, there is art and expression represented in all these examples. Though there are distinct differences in quality, the joy of expression and sharing of self is valid in all forms of art.

The Greek philosopher Aristotle believed that art represents not the "outward appearance of things, but their inward significance." This is an excellent summation of GSE's goals for art and expression within the geriatric group. The art that is produced or examined is for therapeutic, not critical, purposes. Even when the art is created by group members, the intrinsic value is in what is felt (inward significance) more than what is seen by others (outward appearance).

G.L. Lewis (1979) presented an intriguing connection between the Adlerian concepts of humans as striving toward social regard, love, and work as essential to understanding the needs of institutionalized elders. The desire to work and be productive is both instinctive and socially promoted by their generation (the work ethic). Therapeutic art activities can replace work as a new means of being productive. Considering that the word art is derived from the Latin "ars," meaning "skill," this connection between art and work touches a key conflict of aging represented in the loss of work as a means of self-expression and validation.

Art for Elder Groups

The socializing aspect of art in geriatric group work is as significant as its product. By comparison, consider children's art groups in which the focus is on cooperating to produce an art project. This cooperative creativity tends to reduce feelings of isolation and foster a sense of belonging (Swenson, 1991). Harlan (1993) applied that same spirit of using art for connection and reminiscence for persons with Alzheimer's disease. Weisberg and Wilder (2001) took art for older adults to a new level in their book, *Expressive Arts with Elders.* Johnson and Sullivan-Marx (2006) applied similar concepts that they describe as a "unique opportunity to help elderly clients engage in the creative process to facilitate communication, manage emotions and engage in the process of life review." The American Art Therapy Association, International Art Therapy Organization, and Dr. Linda Levine Madori's Therapeutic Thematic Arts Program (TTAT) are some of the many new programs for art with older adults, including those with cognitive impairments. GSE groups have found the same results of cooperation and personal satisfaction for art modalities in elder groups.

The approaches to art therapy are both active (creating art) and passive (responding to art). Depending on the group's dexterity and interest, this may include (a) viewing and discussing classic art reprints; (b) drawing, painting, or clay sculpting; and (c) making collages on a theme or as an expression of feelings. The types of activities can be varied or repeated for maximum effect. Each approach offers commonalities of socialization, response, and reaction as well as differences in application, involvement, and emotional content. Less hands-on applications of the visual arts in group are nonetheless expressive because the works of others are presented.

As with bibliotherapy, art can be a means of seeing beyond the self or seeing the self from a distance. For even cognitively impaired members, art evokes memories or feelings of tranquility and familiarity. Art gives a voice to those who have become nonverbal, particularly older adults with cognitive impairments. Care must be taken with cognitively impaired groups to present a project that is not multistep or overly complex. On the other hand, too much freedom without some direction can lead to "frustration, regression and further agitation" (Johnson & Sullivan-Marx, 2006). These group members are easily frustrated with cognitive-based activities and are often more attentive to the pleasure of the sensory and affective aspects of visual arts (Johnson, Lahey, & Shore, 1992). Art can penetrate the cognitive confusion of Alzheimer's disease and comparable conditions to provide a nonverbal means for expressing emotions and counteracting social isolation in ways that are stimulating without overloading capacity (Weisberg & Wilder, 2001).

The Leader's Role

In art and expression groups, masterful technique is not a factor for either the leader or the group. Leaders do not have to be great artists to apply this modality. Whenever possible, consultation or coleadership with a trained art therapist is highly beneficial. The leader may also find technical assistance from a community volunteer or a college art student who can help organize the supplies, demonstrate projects, and guide group members in completing their artwork. Never be hesitant to learn a new art technique along with the group. Allow the group to encourage each other and the leader while facing the common problem of struggling with running watercolors and misplaced paint spots.

Always be aware of group members' skills, dexterity, vision, and cognitive level in order to match their capabilities to the project and the tools. For example, two GSE art groups enjoyed finger painting but disdained painting with brushes. A revelation while at the hardware store selecting brushes to paint wood trim resulted in a group leader buying a handful of 1-inch and 2-inch brushes for the group. The next brush painting session was enjoyed by all. What was the magic? The larger interior house painting brushes were easier to hold and control, thus making the project less irritating than with the typical, smaller fine art brushes. If preparation time and cleanup are factors, consider using large washable markers instead of paint brushes.

Another useful in vivo experience was learning to offer a smaller number of very distinct colors for each project. Depending on visual acuity, pastels and pale colors are difficult for some elders to distinguish whereas primary colors and bold derivatives are easier to perceive. Preparation is another important aspect. Inform the group, community center, or nursing staff in advance of painting, sculpting, or drawing sessions, which can be messy. Spills and drops happen even for experienced artists. Bring plastic or fabric art aprons for each member to prevent the crisis of ruining a favorite garment. Also take precautions to protect the floor, and cover art tables with old newspapers or inexpensive plastic drop cloths.

In responding to the group projects, the rule is that the effort is even more valuable than the result. Elder art done with shaking hands or reduced vision can be as much a reflection of feelings or words that cannot be verbalized as the work of master artists. In sharing their work, the group's emotions may run extremely high, and inner conflicts may surface; or it can be a playful, relaxing time. Leaders need to be prepared for both possibilities.

Expressive Art: Emotions Reflected in Art

Goals: Finding emotion in art requires bringing to the surface one's own feelings.

Process: The leader shows photos or slides of great paintings in which there is strong emotional content. Avoid showing art in which the strong emotional content is violent or fearful. Take time to allow each group member to view the visual image and think about it. Ask for comments on what the message communicates to each person. What emotions are visible? Do emotions seem to fit the overall situation shown in the image? What emotions are felt by the viewer?

Outcomes: Feeling the strong feelings captured by the artist can be safer than expressing one's own feelings.

Equipment list: Color photos, video projector or computer with large screen. Note: Local museums, colleges, and libraries may loan a collection for viewing.

Expressive Art: Painting

Goals: A way to appreciate painting is to try it firsthand.

Process: The leader or an artistically talented volunteer explains each step of the project. The idea is not to make a great painting but to feel what an artist feels when combining colors on a blank canvas. An assistant or another group member can help guide the hands of a person with limited dexterity or a visual impairment. The visually impaired person may prefer to finger paint, enjoying the feel of applying the paint on canvas. (Note: be certain to use paints that are safe and suitable for finger painting.) Talk about the sensory aspects of mixing the colors, touching the paints, and spreading paint on the surface. Make swirls, dabs, dots, and lines with paint. Anyone can create a simple design such as a rainbow and clouds. Emphasize that the opportunity to feel that how a painting is done is more important than the completed picture.

Outcomes: The outcome here is not the finished picture but the actual experience of painting. Group members often surprise themselves in finding this enjoyable.

Equipment list: Poster paints, watercolors, or finger paints. Small canvas or art paper. Brushes with wide or easy-grip handles and cleanup supplies

Expressive Art: Paint the Music

Goals: Painting as a means for expressing feelings about music.

Process: The leader brings instrumental music recordings with different tempos and styles (i.e., classical, swing, slow jazz, and waltz). The group is instructed to listen to the music, and paint any form, color, or design that gives a visual image to the sounds. There is no pressure to create a picture. The intent is for each person to relate colors with sounds and forms with musical style. The music is changed at regular intervals, 5–10 minutes per interval. Individuals can choose to paint on one poster board or use separate boards for each musical tempo. As the music plays, the leader periodically and softly reminds the group of the objective: to hear and feel the music, then find the colors and forms to express those feelings. In a follow-up session, invite members to show their paintings. Talk about what kind of images each person gets from different types of music. Do sharp lines, zigzag lines, smooth curves, or angles relate to a certain musical style? How can bright, as opposed to dark, colors be used to match musical passages? Did painting the music give way to any new feelings about the music?

Outcomes: Painting and music are additional ways to stimulate expressing feelings. Higher-functioning groups are more successful at completing this project and understanding the connection between feelings and form. However, low-functioning groups enjoy painting to music with less direction and more freeform.

Equipment list: Poster paint, watercolors, or finger paints. Either 11-inch by 17-inch or quarter-size poster board or art paper. Brushes with wide or easy-grip handles and cleanup supplies. Audio recordings of background music with varied tempos and appropriate speakers.

Expressive Art: Soft Sculpture

Goals: A way to understand sculpture is to experience it firsthand.

Process: The leader displays photos or examples of sculptures to the group. To experience the sculptor's feelings at making something from a shapeless mass, each member is given a container of soft dough. Initially, direct each person to squeeze, pat, or roll the dough with his or her eyes closed, thinking only of the sensory perceptions. Using the dough, the leader shows how to roll three sections into balls and stack to resemble a snowman. The leader asks everyone to make a sculpture of anything. Cooking cutters are passed around the table for use in the project for those who seem intimidated by unstructured creativity. Before finishing, affix each project to a block base and label with the artist's name. With the artist's permission, keep the projects in the group room to enjoy, or display them in the community room.

Outcomes: Adults have just as much fun with soft dough projects as children. The result is not as important as the variety of sensory, visual, and creative stimuli that accompany this project.

Equipment list: Children's soft dough material in various colors. Cookie cutters in many shapes. A small wooden block as base for each soft sculpture. Pictures or examples of sculpture.

Expressive Art: Scene Drawn by Group

Goals: The group cooperates to produce a creative project.

Process: As a visual demonstration of cooperation and creativity, the group produces a large scene, with each person making a contribution. Before beginning, the leader explains the basic steps of deciding what type of scene and elements of it. Members work individually or as teams on different areas of the scene. Any members with artistic talent and interest are encouraged to help direct the project. For example, the group decides to create a country scene. A light pencil line is drawn to distinguish middle ground and background. The group discusses what elements best display the country feeling: winding road, bridge, barn, farmhouses, orchard, crops in a field, windmill, and so forth. Each member is assigned a part in the picture. Even physically challenged members can participate, with assistance in guiding their hands to create sweeping clouds or dab red dots for apples on the trees. To avoid tiring the group, work with the paper or poster board on tables. After the work is complete, tape it to the wall for all to appreciate. This project may take several group sessions or with a simple scene may be done in teams in one session.

Outcomes: This project gets everyone involved in decision making, creating, and performing the role of an artist. Working together builds group cohesiveness.

Equipment list: Wide roll of white art or poster board panels. Crayons or washable markers.

Expressive Art: Seasonal Collage

Goals: The group creates a second collage, combining various materials to express a common theme.

Process: The leader talks briefly about the season that is the subject of this group. Reading a poem or listening to related music further establishes images of the season. Group members gather around tables, working in pairs or groups of four. Each mini-group discusses how to express the seasonal theme in a positive way. For example, spring may be portrayed by one group as a "time of renewal" and by another group as "flower fantasy." Each mini-group is directed to use any or all of the items available to communicate their chosen theme with colors and materials in a collage. While working, the leader engages members in discussing how they play to use certain materials, texture combinations, or colors to convey a feeling. Lower-functioning groups often work better separately with clear, simple instructions from the leader and given theme. With all groups, the leader can use volunteers to assist in cutting, gluing, or operating the hot glue gun as members work. This speeds up the project and is safer. This project can be done over several sessions. Plan a final or follow-up session as a presentation time for the group to view and comment on what they feel or see in each other's work.

Outcomes: Translating feelings into a collage does not require artistic skill or a high degree of digital dexterity. This three-dimensional, multitextured collage is a satisfying sensory experience with a creative result.

Equipment list: Wide roll of white art paper or poster board. Crayons or washable markers, scissors, and glue. Old magazines for cutouts or precut pictures, fabric pieces, ribbon, beads, leaves, and twigs. Sponges with poster paints are used for overlay and accents.

Expressive Art: Circles and Forms

Goals: Members use shapes to express feelings of inclusion or exclusion.

Process: On a large marker board, the leader draws examples of how shapes and colors can represent concepts. For example, circles intertwined show a bond as with beads in a chain or symbolize people linking arms and walking together. Give pencils, paper, and templates to each member. Let them practice outlining the templates with pencils. Then give each a sheet of clean paper, and direct each person to select a form (circle, square, triangle) that represents themselves. They draw that form in the top area of the blank page and color it with a color that expresses how they feel today, then select one or two forms (same or different) that represent other group members. These forms are drawn near or just below the form for self and colors for these forms assigned. On the lower part of the page or on a clean page, each person uses the forms to show the self in relation to this group. The actual number of forms and group members is not important. What is significant is looking at the individual's feelings about inclusion in or exclusion from this group. After everyone is finished, talk generally about how it feels to be part of a group. What makes them feel accepted? How do other people communicate acceptance to them in nonverbal ways? Drawing self and the group can be done by a person at any functioning level. Using the drawings as a springboard to discussion of intergroup relationships is suitable only for higher-functioning members in groups who have some cohesiveness or have spent a longer time together.

Outcomes: The leader learns much about each member's sense of belonging from the design and colors used in these drawings. Members whose work shows separation from others, dismal colors or forms, and overall feelings of discomfort need individual attention from the leader before continuing in group.

Equipment list: Templates in several forms and sizes. Colored pencils or large writing pencils. Marker board.

Expressive Art: Sponge Painting

Goals: Simple sponge painting requires minimal skill and produces interesting expressions of color and form.

Process: Workstations with supplies are prepared for each group member around a table. The leader demonstrates how to use the sponges for painting by dropping them into the paint and then onto the paper. Group members are directed to use the sponge shapes and letters to cover the blank surface with an original design that is personally appealing.

Outcomes: This project is simple to do with or without artistic ability. The color blending and shapes may be very well defined or random, according to individual style. Completing the project is entertaining and offers some sensory stimulation.

Equipment list: Precut sponges in various shapes and letters. Half-size poster board or quarter yard of strong, tight-weave cloth. Disposable pie tins or recycled margarine containers, washable paints. Cleanup supplies.

Expressive Art: Pain Management

Goals: Using drawing to express and manage physical pain.

Process: Many elders suffer from some level of physical decline or pain. With reduced activity, an excessive amount of attention is given to discomfort rather than to establishing a sense of mastery. The leader initiates this project by discussing how difficult it is to explain pain. Using the marker board and colored markers, the leader illustrates a common pain description such as "a red-hot sun, with sharp rays extending all around." Engage the group in a discussion of what moderates the sun's heat. One option is to draw blue clouds around the sun and cover the rays with raindrops. This is a cooling image that makes the heat more manageable. Instruct each person to draw a shape, form, or color that represents pain on the paper. As each person presents his or her pain drawing, the group brainstorms ideas for another image to moderate the pain. After everyone draws a cooling or soothing image over the pain picture, discuss how this visualization can be used to master pain.

Outcomes: This visualization exercise supported by art reinforces a sense of control that is often a critical issue for elders.

Equipment list: Art paper, drawing pencils and crayons, or washable markers. Marker board.

Expressive Art: Message in the Masters

Goals: Group members explore nonverbal messages communicated through great works of art.

Process: The leader introduces this activity as a group effort to identify the obvious and hidden meanings in well-known artwork. This activity is more effective after the group has done some painting or other creative project. View a picture, consider the name of the work, and what is apparent at first glance. For example, Leonardo da Vinci's *Mona Lisa* is a familiar image. The painting of the woman and her famous smile are well known, but does she actually seem happy? If not happiness, what other emotion might be behind her smile? What does the landscape scene in the background tell about this woman or her life? Are there any other elements in the picture that communicate a message? These are examples of questions that stimulate discussion on what group members see and feel about each picture. The leader may write summary comments on the marker board or keep the discussion free flowing. Continue with this format to discuss several art prints from different historical periods and styles.

Outcomes: For some members, classic art is pleasurable and stimulates memories of times and places from their past. Visual acuity is a greater hurdle than cognitive functioning in participating in this activity. Shorter attention spans of lower-functioning groups suggest that discussion remain on a general level—the obvious subjects in the picture and feelings derived from viewing it.

Equipment list: Library book, prints, or digital pictures of well-known art by da Vinci, Renoir, Monet, and other master artists.

Phototherapy

The image is for us the way to the original; in it we touch at least the hem of the garment of the eternal idea.

Odo Casel

How many words is a picture worth? Capturing a moment in time or a visual image of a feeling, pictures can stimulate a thousand words or a dozen unspoken emotions. Phototherapy is to the eyes what bibliotherapy is to the mind. The concept of phototherapy in the medical realm is linked with using different light spectrums to treat sunlight-deprived persons for such maladies as seasonal affective disorder. With the GSE modality, phototherapy brings to light memories, ideas, and social interaction.

Phototherapy is an emerging specialty with many connections to art therapy. An image captured on film can be a stark black-and-white representation of an event from the morning newspaper or an artistic photo that is lovely, colorful, and abstract enough to be open to interpretation. Both of these types of photos are useful in phototherapy.

Family photo albums as well as unrelated photos of others can be used with elder groups to encourage communication, process feelings at a safe distance, and recall memories. These snapshots are captured moments in time. Photos show things as they are compared with memories that recall things with or without personal interpretation. Colors in a photo come from impressions on the film as interpreted at the processing lab or altered by filters and special effects. Emotions, beliefs, thoughts, background, and other abstract elements are impressions that color memories in individual and stylized ways. Experience this difference by finding an old photo of a family event. Ask two or three other people who were in the photo (or present at the event) to tell the story of what happened. The reports may have a little in common as agreeing that dinner was held at Grandma's house. Beyond that, the actual images are personalized by being "filtered" through each person's beliefs, feelings, and attitudes. Memories as snapshots of the mind are often not as clear or as accurate as snapshots taken with a nonemotional camera.

Leaders need to be aware that elders from some cultural backgrounds are resistant to working with photos as they are too personal or an invasion of private space. Such attitudes may be related to historical views by some American Indian and African groups who feel that having a photo taken could compromise their spiritual being. Elders of various cultural heritages are likely to respond adversely to photos depicting violence, interpersonal conflict, or destruction. The harsh realism of today's typical news photos are both disturbing and threatening to persons who grew up in an area where photos were simple, less available, and treasured possessions.

How to Use Photos in Group

Phototherapy with elders is less concerned with checking on the absolute truth of memories than with using the images to clarify and enrich memories with emotional, sensory, and relationship details. As an affective modality, the amount of photo stimulus is carefully monitored to avoid overwhelming elders. Photos of self or family offer a low-key means of examining false beliefs (i.e., "always the ugly duckling" or "never spent time with my children"). Photos of personally significant events (graduation, marriage, birthdays, holidays) stimulate the feelings of belonging and achievement.

When photos of the group members are not available, the leader can substitute photos of unrelated others that represent comparable times, events, or life stages. Magazines are full of colorful pictorial advertisements. Leaders interested in the modality need to keep adding to a collection of old photos gathered from family and friends. Another great way to add to the collection is by buying old photo albums at garage sales and thrift stores where a few dollars can purchase a full album or box of old photos. The local historical society is another source of copies of photos or borrowed slide shows.

Non-Identified Photos

The non-identified photos can be effective as those that are identified. A photo of a young 1940s Army nurse may receive such varied reactions as "She reminds me of my sister who left home to join the nurses corps," "she's the cheerful nurse who cared for me at the VA hospital," or "she's like so many brave young women who did their part for the war effort." This is more than a game of "let's pretend." It's an exercise in expanding on what is seen in the picture with what the image means to the observer. Particularly with cognitively impaired groups, there is a greater freedom to draw assumptions about the non-identified person's name, age, lifestyle, and personality. There is also less frustration or pressure to recognize people who are vaguely familiar as is often true with photos of family or older peers.

Phototherapy also works well with nonverbal and verbally limited elders. Simple photos with clear, distinct facial expressions can be used to inquire about feelings or mood. The leader may present two or three (but no more) choices showing a same-sex person who is smiling, pensive, or sad, then ask the elder to point to the one that "feels like you feel today." A variation on this is for the leader to look at several photos with the elder and observe those photos to which he or she is attracted.

Phototherapy pioneer Judy Weiser (2002), who launched the Photo Therapy Center in Vancouver, Canada, and its online component (www.phototherapy-centre.com) identified Five Techniques of Phototherapy that include the following: Client takes the photo, Client is subject of photo, Client takes a self-portrait, Client in a Family Album, and Photo Projective. With community groups that have more mobility, the group leader could ask members to be the photographer and take pictures or make a self-portrait to bring back to group. For groups with mobility limitations or cognitive impairment, the photos used will be primarily those from family albums including those where the group member is the subject of the photo or photos of unidentified persons. Group leaders will also use photos of nature, places, events, and seasons as part of phototherapy.

Phototherapy Groups

Phototherapy: Tell a Picture Story—Magazines

Goals: The picture is a springboard for reminiscence or expression of feelings.

Process: The leader opens with comments on how every picture tells a story without words. Using a color ad or photo, the leader displays it and gives his or her own impressions of the story behind it. Then each group member is given a different color picture to study. Going around the group, each person shows the picture and tells the picture story as she or he sees it. The leader may ask less verbal questions to help them focus on the picture story. A newer group or low-functioning group may work from the same picture. Together, each member can contribute observations that the leader summarizes on a marker board to tell the picture story. The best pictures for this activity are those with a single action and easy-to-recognize objects. The pictures that elicit the most detailed or personalized response in GSE groups are those with one or two children playing, a family in the home, a tranquil garden, or babies.

Outcomes: Elders at all levels of functioning can become involved in this interpretive, projective activity. Many responses are general and evident from the pictures. Other members, particularly cognitively impaired ones, are prompted by the pictures to personalize responses and reveal vivid experiences or feelings.

Equipment list: Cut out large color advertisements or photos from magazines and paste each on sturdy cardboard. Marker board and boldly colored markers.

Phototherapy: Tell a Picture Story—Family Albums

Goals: Pictures of self and family are part of reminiscences and reality checks.

Process: Before group or at the first session of a series, the leader explains how familiar photos will be the center of this activity and asks each person to bring personal photos or albums. If possible, have each person bring at least one photo of him- or herself as a small child, teenager, young adult, or older adult. Another theme for this group is magic moments such as family holidays, graduation, marriage, birth or adoption of child, and activities with friends. With higher-functioning groups, have each member describe him- or herself at specific ages or stages before showing the photos. In GSE groups, a woman who claimed to never have been included in family events was seen in several photos looking content amid relatives. Another man who said that his son never spent time with him is seen in photos of the two of them fishing, bowling, and rebuilding a boat. Through photos, one can confront myths or false beliefs about the individual's relationship to family and friends. On the positive side, photos affirm connections between generations, siblings, and friends as well as show continuity. Lower-functioning groups manage well with reminiscences and feelings evoked from photos yet are less likely to develop new insights.

Outcomes: Personal photos are a pictorial history that are sometimes more accurate than memories and family legends. These photos become vehicles for closure, resolution, and affirmation.

Equipment list: Family photos of each member. It's best to use larger photos or enlarge their size on a photocopier.

Phototherapy: Autobiographical Photo Collage

Goals: This activity gives visual introduction over the life span.

Process: This exercise requires two or three sessions and some additional volunteer assistance for group members. Several weeks before beginning, ask members to locate five to seven photos of themselves at various ages and with important people from their past and present. Or get approval to send a letter to each member's family requesting photos. Also, obtain approval from the facility to hang the finished collage on or outside the door to each person's room. The leader introduces the project and briefly outlines the steps to completion. Writing the steps in large print on poster board is a helpful reference. The leader can go around the table and work with each person separately or involve the group in reviewing everyone's photos. Assist with trimming photos for fit and balance. The leader can take a quick-developing photo of each member as the centerpiece of the collage. Around the perimeter, other photos are arranged. The member prints a caption on plain paper and glues it below the collage. This allows for errors. Or an assistant can write the caption as dictated by the individual. If the group can work and converse, talk about recollections from the photos and relationships with other people in those pictures. Lower-functioning members and those with limited vision will need more assistance and a slower pace. When the collage is finished, insert it in a frame, and ask each member to present and describe his or her autobiographical collage.

Outcomes: As a mini-photo history, this collage is a source of pleasure and identity reaffirmation to each person daily as well as a way for staff to relate better to residents. Any time the collage is complimented by visitors, the resident feels pride in having completed the project.

Equipment list: Plain poster board cut to fit inside an 8 × 10 or 11 × 17 clear plastic, nonbreakable frame. Safety scissors. Precut construction paper borders. Colorful stickers. Paper on which to write captions. Glue or photo-mounting corners. Disposable camera.

Phototherapy: American Life Photo Essays

Goals: Looking at people and places that are part of the American scene that are similar to and different than an individual's experiences.

Process: The leader may open with a Walt Whitman verse or other words that focus on Americana. Ask each group member to name the state or region in which they grew up or where they lived most of their life. Point out the areas on a U.S. map. Then begin to explore the pictures in a photo essay book. Focus on themes, ages, people, places, or activities. As in the "tell a picture story" activities, have each member comment on the story behind the photo. Then read the caption or explanation from the book. Encourage group members to share memories of similar scenes from the past or present experiences.

Outcomes: Great photos are compelling and mentally stimulating. Responses may be directed toward the actual photo content or the memory accessed because of the photo.

Equipment list: Coffee-table-sized color photo books from the library or similar photos on color slides. If using slides, get a slide projector and large screen. A national map.

Phototherapy: A Feeling Collage

Goals: Using photos of non-identified persons and places to display a range of feelings.

Process: The leader begins by showing some very emotive photos and seeking the group's response on what they feel when viewing each photo. Choose some very clear images such as the famous victory kiss of a sailor and a nurse at the close of World War II. Give a set of pictures to each group member to review. Instruct them to keep any photos that show an emotion they recently felt (or currently feel). Collect the discards and distribute to other group members. Allow one or two sessions to review and choose emotive photos. When every member has at least five photos, distribute poster board. Depending on their dexterity, members can trim photos themselves or with assistance. Arrange photos on the board in any order desired. Members can write feeling words on the poster board or glue on preprinted words. The leader gets, ahead of time, copies of large-type emotive words (i.e., love, anger, sad, happy, or confused) with an ample supply for participants. Be very nondirective in each person's choice of photos. One person will have all happy photos, and another will choose tense scenes. Invite (but don't require) each person to talk about the collage and its meaning. Display the completed collages in the community room.

Outcomes: Emotional responses to photos can be safer to express than verbal admissions. Cognitively impaired persons are occasionally better able to reveal themselves by the visual-emotional connection than with a verbal-emotional response.

Equipment list: Old magazines, catalogs, or news photos. Safety scissors. Poster board. Glue.

Phototherapy: Faces of Children

Goals: Recall the wonders of childhood and parental feelings of sharing those moments of discovery.

Process: The leader tells a brief story or reads an essay with a very vivid description of a childhood event and emotional responses. The group is asked to consider how much of a child's feelings are evident in facial expressions. Then each member is given a picture involving a child. After a pause to study the pictures, group members present their photos and tell about the action and what the emotions show. With each presentation, the leader asks if anyone can share a time that they saw a child in such a situation. How much of the child's feelings do they understand? What would they like to say to the child?

Outcomes: Elders are frequently removed from children and enjoy even a photo glimpse of their playful, forthright behaviors. Acting as the child's advocate, some elders will connect with feelings and unresolved issues of their inner child, which is more distantly projected onto the photo.

Equipment list: Pictures of children of various ages and ethnicity and with various facial expressions. May also use the therapeutic poster of children's emotions. Brief story or essay about a childhood event.

Phototherapy: Travel by Photo

Goals: Armchair travel is without physical or financial limitations yet brings exotic places within reach of the imagination.

Process: Before group, the leader collects colorful photos and related objects and packs them in a suitcase to be unpacked at group. It may be possible to borrow a slide show or video from a local travel agent or auto club. You may also get an experienced commentator along with the show. Another option is to record a TV or cable travel show or documentary. Arrange chairs in rows as on an airplane or in a v-wing configuration so everyone gets a good view. As the group gathers, distribute the homemade passports that have a list of several locations. For higher-functioning groups, the leader gives several clues about today's travel itinerary. Then for all groups, name the location and point to it on the map or globe before beginning the presentation. For lower-functioning groups, interrupt the show approximately every 10 minutes and discuss what was seen. This compensates for short attention spans. Even with higher-functioning groups, avoid videos exceeding 25–30 minutes. Allow time to discuss what was seen and anything new learned from this armchair trip. Then the leader stamps and dates the passport and tells of plans to see one of the other locations listed.

Outcomes: Travel is said to broaden a person's horizons. In this group, armchair travel allows members to journey in their imaginations to places they are not likely to go or recall places they have previously been. Focusing on the differences in colors, sights, textures, people, buildings, and tourist attractions is both entertaining and informative.

Equipment list: Travel posters, brochures, and books. Photos and related objects packed in a suitcase. Map or globe. Slides or video presentation. A homemade passport or postcard souvenir. A date stamp or symbol stamp (available in stationery stores and children's toy stores).

Phototherapy: Holiday Images

Goals: Present a more vibrant view of the holiday and differing methods of celebration.

Process: Christmas, Thanksgiving, New Year's, Valentine's Day, Memorial Day, and Fourth of July are excellent subjects for this phototherapy activity. A few weeks before the stated holiday or during the week of the holiday, the group views photos of celebrations and discusses the scenes. The leader may show photos of past and present events, similar holidays around the world, or children at holidays as focal point for this discussion. GSE leaders were surprised that a high-functioning group wanted to discuss how they celebrated Christmas during World War II.

After searching the library, photo essay books were located with scenes of both battlefields and family back home. Rather than being depressed by the subject, the group radiated in sharing how their feelings of hope transcended the circumstances. From that reminiscence came a renewed spirit of refusing to be limited by things outside the self. The therapeutic implications of this session for coping with present problems was far beyond anything GSE leaders planned. Don't be afraid to mix photos of various emotions and situations in holiday scenes.

Outcomes: Holidays are packed with nostalgia and recurrent feelings of loss as well as happiness and excitement. With minimal involvement in holiday plans, some elders choose to emotionally disengage. Allowing expression of positive and negative feelings, group members can find new meanings for holidays and ideally create a family and a celebration among themselves.

Equipment list: Photos or slides of holiday activities, food, clothing, and people engaged in traditional holiday activities. Recycled holiday card photos.

Phototherapy: Mature Images

Goals: Challenge negative views of aging that are ingrained by our youth-centered society.

Process: The leader begins by asking members to give their definitions of attractiveness for men and women. What characteristics show dignity, strength, and pride? Show a series of photos of older men and women either in prints or on slides. Then show the series again, stopping to discuss characteristics of each photo. The leader writes the descriptions on the marker board in a positive column or negative column. Positive descriptions are timeless (e.g., lovely, distinguished, confident). Negative descriptions are often age defaming (e.g., tired, wrinkled, stooped). Return to the photos that were described negatively. Encourage the group to find another, positive way to describe the image. The "tired" face can also be "dedicated to helping others." The leader can also present photos of senior adult magazine models. Ask the group to debate whether elder models are attractive because of their age or because they look younger.

Outcomes: If teenagers seek every mirror, elders shun them. Learning to see beauty in the aging body is a means of acceptance that can increase participation in self-care.

Equipment list: Photos, slides, or photo essay books featuring older men and women of various ages, socioeconomic status, health, mobility, and emotional expressions. Marker board.

Phototherapy: News Images

Goals: Looking at current events through the photographer's eyes.

Process: This is another way to bring current events into the overall group agenda. The leader scans news sources for major stories and human interest stories accompanied by photos. Begin by inquiring about any major or breaking news event such as a hurricane, earthquake, congressional vote, or trial. Show related photos and discuss how effectively the story is portrayed in the pictures. Then present the less-promoted human interest stories (e.g., a fire rescue, three generations graduate together, or a new community theater company). Without revealing the headline or the text, ask members what they think the story is about from looking at the picture. After a few guesses, read the text. Members can comment on how well or how poorly the picture tells the story.

Outcomes: In this activity, members gain information and use analytical skills.

Equipment list: Larger news photos from newspapers or magazines mounted on poster board with the story printed in larger type.

9

GROUP MODALITIES
FOR THE SPIRIT

The creation and preservation of values; that is what gives meaning to our civilization, and the participation in this is what gives significance, ultimately, to the individual human life.

Lewis Mumford

The beliefs held and practiced by an individual are outward expressions of spirituality. In approaching the final Eriksonian stage of Integrity v. Despair (Erikson, 1950), it is customary for older adults to reflect on the meaning and legacy of their lives. Part of that meaning and legacy for many is in their spiritual expression. Spirituality is not limited to a philosophy, denomination, or label. The Park, Zimmerman, Kinslow, Shin, and Roff (2012) study of social engagement within assisted living adults found that maintaining connections with members of the elder's former church affiliation as well as having the ability to attend religious services inside or outside the facility remained of high importance to residents. Older adults are nearing the end of life, which leaves them to face whether they believe in life after death or the complete end of existence at death. Science does not provide the answer. In seeking peace about this question, older adults have to come to terms with their spirituality and decide how to finish life based on those beliefs. Because of the existential crisis faced as the end of life draws near, spiritual expression can be an emotional support and a positive factor in reducing depression (Turesky & Schultz, 2010). Tornstam (1989, 2005) expanded his theory of "gerotranscendence" to go beyond traditional religion and determine how the individual relates as a spiritual being within the tangible universe.

As part of a holistic program, the spirit is an integral part of the mind-body-social-spirit whole. For that reason, GSE programs include modalities for the spirit. In a review of 13 studies on spirituality, Dalby (2006) discovered that interest in spiritual matters is likely to increase rather than decrease with older ages. Lee's (2011) study on spirituality and religious influence found that older adults with strongest spiritual experiences also had lower levels of anxiety, greater vitality, and an overall greater sense of well-being. In providing the group as a safe place to talk about spirituality, older adults have the opportunity to process their concerns that may not have been given attention by family or friends. Lewis (2001) suggests that the therapeutic value of spirituality may become increasingly important as it resonates with the new elders—the Baby Boomers. Whether in formal religious rites or acts of daily living, values and roles over a lifetime are part of spiritual expression and beliefs about self, life, and others.

Exploring Values and Roles

A meaningful element of life satisfaction is derived from the roles filled and the values dearly held over a lifetime. Each group member arrives with a collection of established values and roles (both positive and negative). These long-held attitudes and personal experiences form the basis for this modality of self-discovery and social interaction. Regardless of how many values or roles are shared, different themes emerge that are integral to reinforce self-esteem. Exploring values and roles is a reflective, existential modality that searches for meaning from the past as a sustaining force for a time-limited and uncertain future.

Values

The significance of values as an expression of unity between the mind and the heart was recognized by John Dewey (1939). Years later, the quest was revived by Maslow (1959) and Rogers (1961) as important to the psychosocial development of each person. In looking at the origin of values, Piaget (1965) explained that the earliest childhood encounter with value development comes in two stages: *moral realism*, the reality of rules; and *moral relativism*, the potential to changes rules. Kohlberg (1963) expanded Piaget's stages into a theory of moral development with three levels (pre-moral, role conformity, and self-accepted morality) and seven stages. The stages in the third level constitute an ongoing series of decisions about individual rights, dictates of conscience, and individual actions as part of a universal ethic. Bathed in the afterglow of the humanist movement, Raths, Hamin, and Simon (1966) created a controversial approach known as *values clarification* to be used in schools. As the popularity of values clarification grew, its application was expanded to include adults from corporate team building to a less academically inclined method of teaching courses intended to loosely resemble philosophy.

The Exploring Values and Roles modality is an adaptation of values clarification with elders that is called *values solidification*. Among Raths et al.'s (1966) criteria for a clarified value are that it be "cherished, claimed publicly, and consistently practiced." GSE groups begin with the assumption that senior adults have enough life experience to know what values they hold. Even cognitively impaired elders retain much of their values or life rules in a very concrete way, although they may no longer be able to deal with the information in an abstract, philosophical manner. Regardless of formal education, the oldest-old have less difficulty articulating their values than do the new-old, their Baby Boomer children. The middle to oldest adults in our geriatric groups are clear about the work ethic that they learned at an early age to practice with a self-reliant, can-do creed. Work with them to identify and recapture the positive feelings emanating from adherence to those values.

Roles

For many older adults, who you are and what you do are synonymous. Job descriptions were short and simple for persons coming of age to work in post-Depression America. There were white-collar industrialists, blue-collar laborers, soil-collared farmers, and homeless persons who lost both shirts and their collars. Women were either the white-gloved ladies of the house or their white-aproned servants. Workers, predominately men, found a job with the goal of a secure paycheck and hoping to receive a plaque and a gold watch at retirement.

In a similarly structured style, relationships were predictable. The social rules dictated a lifelong monogamous marriage with children. Grandparents were treated with profound respect and were often cared for in the homes of their adult children. This was a time in which family values were prized, and most people were in agreement about the nature of those values. Coming from such a predictable social order, today's elders must feel like Dorothy, hit by a ton of bricks and wondering if they are in Kansas. The rigid role definitions that they expected seem to vanish at the time they enter a bewildering period that Blau (1973) called *role exit* when stable patterns of socialization and meaning cease. The elder is no longer a parent, coworker, or resident of the same neighborhood. Add to that the deaths of a spouse and of family or friends, and the individual faces a series of losses that rip apart lifetime attachments. New roles emerge, yet even those roles are often restricted by mobility, illness, isolation, and financial reversal. The geriatric group leader must understand the significance of roles in the life of elders. There are many strengths and characteristics to be discovered about the roles of a lifetime. A 70-year-old man comes to mind who insisted that he had "never amounted to anything." During an exploration of values and roles, he found a side of himself that he had never before recognized. He had long "felt guilty staying home with his mother and sisters during World War II." In reality, he was the only male left at home to help support the family, as his father had been killed in the early months of fighting, and his three older brothers had enlisted. As the group talked about what kinds of things he did every day and how he helped his family, a different picture developed. He finally acknowledged that he had been the man of the house, keeping the roof repaired and working extra hours to buy his sister's graduation dress. Seeing this critical young adult role as important was the key to looking at the positive aspects of subsequent life roles.

Values and Roles for the Group

At a time when roles are diminishing for elders, membership in the group becomes a new role that is tailored to present circumstances. Understanding the values and roles that have sustained an elder to this point provides important clues to effective coping in aging. Looking for elements of life satisfaction and current ability to deal with aging are part of restoring or discovering a new level of self-esteem. This is an intense process from which the most lasting results are derived by groups with greater levels of cohesion. In a less intense application, this is suitable as an anchor and redirection modality for cognitively impaired groups.

There is no attempt to change or challenge values unless the elder makes that decision independently. Efforts at values solidification are to have each member identify, claim, and find new ways to apply personal values to present living. Along with exploring past roles and the positive elements therein, members are discovering new roles within the group. Highly cohesive groups are particularly amazing in how they create group roles. One very special GSE group decided to redefine their group roles as a family. The oldest man (94) and the oldest woman (92) received consensus as the "parents." The members in their 70s were their children, and two ladies in their 80s felt best as "aunties." Because of her relative youth, a 66-year-old woman became the "baby sister." In case you are wondering what happened to the 30-something group leaders, they were designated "friends." This role assignment surfaced periodically and playfully in a way that all seemed to enjoy. When the baby sister suffered a stroke, her group family showered her with concern and visits. This "role adaptation" was the first of many signs that the new roles in group filled Grand Canyon-sized voids in these people's desire to care about others. If there are such things as dream teams, then this was the "dream geriatric group experience." They enacted Yalom's (1985) belief that the best curative factors in group therapy emerge from the support, acceptance, and hope generated within the group rather than from any therapeutic magic of the leader.

Role: Birth Order

Goals: Consider an individual's role in the family of origin according to birth order.

Process: The leader introduces the topic by asking each group member about the number of siblings and his or her placement in the birth order. Write this information on the marker board (i.e., Mary—third child, first girl). As framework for the discussion, the leader reads segments of literature on birth order, roles, and personality types. A prewritten poster in large lettering giving brief characteristics of the only child, first child, middle child, and youngest child is a helpful reference tool for members. Each member is asked to comment on how she or he conforms to the birth-order assumptions. The discussion can expand to include perceptions of parental favoritism or scapegoating of different siblings.

Outcomes: Birth-order theories are unfamiliar to many elders and generate insights about their place within the family and that of their siblings.

Equipment list: Reference books on birth order, such as Dr. Kevin Leman's *The Birth Order Book* (2009). Poster board charts, marker board, and boldly colored markers.

Role: Beliefs about Families

Goals: Elders have experienced several generations of family life: their grandparents, parents, children, and grandchildren. This topic deals with the imperatives and beliefs about family life and how they have been manifested in several generations.

Process: Leader begins with a discussion of what constitutes a family. As group members formulate this definition, they are asked to describe the ideal family. The leader adds sociological information on how the definition of family has changed during this century by reading about traditional families, blended families, divorced families, single-parent families, adoptive families, and transracial and transcultural families. Members are then asked about how their families changed from their grandparents' generation through that of their adult children and grandchildren. Has anything changed in their families' definition of the role of elder relatives? In society's definition? Is the role of family matriarch or patriarch the same as it was for prior generations? How does each member feel about the changes?

Outcomes: Family beliefs about roles are significant to the way elders are treated. If the family's respect for elders diminished over generations, then the present elders may feel cheated and angry. If the elder role is revered, then there is comfort and respect. Dealing with these feelings is too often minimized by family and caregivers.

Equipment list: None.

Role: Best Friends

Goals: To recapture positive feelings of sharing with friends.

Process: The leader begins by reading a short essay on friendship or telling a positive personal story of an experience with a best friend. Members are given a few quiet moments to recall the friendships that enhanced their lives and tell about their best friends and what made the relationships special. The leader tracks names and comments as each person speaks (i.e., Mark—childhood friend, played baseball together, got measles at the same time). These comments can also be recorded by or for the member on individual pages. After everyone has a turn discussing a best friend, ask members to reflect on a person that they decided to befriend and how this was accomplished. With higher-functioning groups, talk about the risks and benefits of making new friends at this time in life. Brainstorm a plan for approaching another resident and beginning a friendship.

Outcomes: Family is a given; friends are chosen. The persons, circumstances, and results of friendships are indelible experiences from which elders can draw strength and recall feelings of acceptance.

Equipment list: Short essay or article on friendship. Marker board. Paper and pen.

Role: Work or Career

Goals: Look at the importance of work or career in adult life and how to deal with the loss of that role in retirement.

Process: Before group, the leader reads social histories of each member to learn something about prior occupations. Bringing photos or props that symbolize those occupations enhances the discussion. The leader begins this topic by recalling the Horatio Alger work ethic on which most elders were raised. Discuss what the work ethic means to each member. Then become more specific, asking each member to recall his or her first job. What were the duties, and how much was the pay? Who was influential in selecting the type of work (the individual, parents, spouse, teacher)? What type of work was pursued in later years? What was the last job before retirement? How did work outside and inside the home change during their work years? Do they miss working? If each person could return to work now and get any job imaginable, what would that job be? What skills would that job require? High- and low-functioning groups participate well in discussion about work and hold strong feelings about personal productivity linked to the work ethic.

Outcomes: Probing experiences and attitudes toward work tells much about self-image in older adults. The imaginary work question may give clues to activities or skills that an individual may be able to translate into leisure activities.

Equipment list: Occupational photos and props (i.e., firefighter's hat, chalkboard, briefcase, toolbox, or chef's apron).

Role: Parenting or Caregiving

Goals: Consider the importance of being needed as a parent or caregiver.

Process: The leader asks each member to name his or her children or another person for whom he or she had caretaking responsibilities. Discuss the role of parent or caregiver. Ask each member what qualities define a good parent or caregiver. Which of those qualities did they develop while parenting or caregiving? What were the changes in their roles as adults, workers, or spouses that occurred because of parenting or caregiving? Were those changes anticipated or resented?

Did they model their roles after their parents or choose to change how they ful-filled parenting or caregiving roles? What caregiver in their life now is more like their ideal caregiver role and why? How did they show appreciation to this good caregiver? Encourage the group to list on the marker board ways to verbally re-ward good caregiving and appropriately express views of inadequate care.

Outcomes: Moving from the elders' parenting or caregiving roles to expecta-tions and realities about care receiving can aid adjustment to the present situation and identification rather than hostility toward caregivers.

Equipment list: Marker board.

Role: Activities in the Community

Goals: Review how individuals become invested in the larger community and the results of their participation.

Process: The leader displays a poster with concentric circles labeled from the center outward: self, family, neighborhood, school, church, interest group, and city. Bring the poster to each member, point to each circle, and ask members to tell one way to be involved in each area. Talk about the type of activities and level of commitment and satisfaction gained from each activity. Encourage members to compare activities and different ways of contributing to similar aspects of com-munity. In a later or expanded group, discuss present opportunities to partici-pate in their community through residents' council, interest groups, or outside activities.

Outcomes: Recognizing the desire of emotionally healthy adults to participate in a community outside of self and family, motivate members to be as invested as possible in the community within their reach.

Equipment list: Marker board and poster illustration.

Role: Clichés as Imperatives

Goals: Elders grew up with many clichés given as rules. Explore how influential these clichés were in their beliefs and definition of roles.

Process: The leader writes several well-known clichés on the maker board, such as "A stitch in time saves nine"; "Still waters run deep"; "Don't cry over spilled milk"; and "If at first you don't succeed, try, try, try, again." Members are asked to recall other clichés that they frequently heard or said. After collecting ad-ditional statements, ask members to explain in their own words what each cliché means. Discuss differences in meaning. Does the statement express a moral or practical message? How is it used? Are some clichés regional or ethnic in origin? Which clichés reflect or define personal beliefs?

Outcomes: Clichés are a former generation's "shoulds" that restrict behaviors and state imperatives. This exercise encourages thinking about how clichés de-fined an individual's role and beliefs and whether they remain valid for today.

Equipment list: Marker board or preprinted posters. Large-print copies for each member to follow.

Role: Rules to Live By

Goals: Determine how rules were defined, assimilated, and transmitted to individuals and the impact of rules for role definition.

Process: The leader begins with a simple definition of rules and gives several common examples for rules of conduct, for example, the Ten Commandments, the Golden Rule, the Good Samaritan, public laws, and civil rights legislation. Members are asked to name other rules that governed their conduct in their parental home as children and later as adults. The leader lists answers on the marker board. From among the rules listed, each member is given time to tell which were most influential in his or her life and why. This discussion can be expanded to include such topics as which rules did they find fair or unfair in their lives, who made the rules in their homes, how do they feel about the rules that affect them in the present circumstances, and what can they do to change or cope with the rules if they disagree?

Outcomes: Elders are typically a rule-respecting generation; however, that does not imply agreement with rules. This topic allows a nonjudgmental forum to discuss feelings about rules that governed their past and present life.

Equipment list: Marker board.

Role: The Good Neighbor

Goals: In less frantic times, neighbors were a vital part of the family social circle and the primary source of adult interaction for homemakers. This exercise reflects on the role of neighbors and how to recapture it.

Process: The leader begins by reading an essay or showing a video segment of a classic family-oriented show with a positive scene of communication between neighbors. Members are invited to recall and tell of a favorite neighbor. What was special about that person? How did this neighbor help the member's adjustment to a new area? Next, ask how each member acted as a good neighbor to someone else. Discuss the qualities of a good neighbor, which the leader summarizes on the marker board. For higher-functioning groups, refocus this topic to present circumstances. How can they be a good neighbor to another resident in a retirement or nursing home? What can they do with limited resources and mobility to show that they are good neighbors? Would they think differently about living in this facility if they considered it their new neighborhood?

Outcomes: At all levels, members can find satisfaction in recollections of having or being a good neighbor. Challenge higher-functioning groups to find ways to bring the good-neighbor concept to present circumstances.

Equipment list: Essay on or video recording of a classic family-oriented show. Marker board.

Role: The Roles of My Life

Goals: After conducting several role-oriented group topics, this topic crystallizes each person's self-image as influenced by the roles he or she has played in life.

Process: The leader reviews prior group discussions on roles. In creating a list of roles for each person, either work separately to list each person's roles or list key roles and name of each member acknowledging that role. Stimulate recall with basic roles divided by age or stage, for example, member as a youth or child, grandchild, niece or nephew, student, friend, or teammate. In adulthood, roles may include friend, dating partner, spouse, worker, homemaker, business owner, aunt or uncle, and parent. Some later adult roles are friend, grandparent, widow or widower, club member, and retiree. Draw out special interests that add other roles such as artist, sewer, carpenter, cook, gardener, or photographer. Make a list of roles for each person. Even those with low self-esteem who claim to have done nothing important are surprised at how many roles they have filled in life. With higher-functioning groups, expand this topic to discuss ways to amplify or alter present roles. A leader who is aware of community resources and facility programs can help members connect with additional means of role fulfillment.

Outcomes: This in an effective self-esteem-building exercise for those at all levels of functioning.

Equipment list: Marker board and personal inventory sheets.

Spirituality

> The spiritual life does not remove us from the world but leads us deeper into it.
>
> Henri Nouwen

Reaching the seventh and eighth decade prompts most elders to contemplate their future beyond this lifetime. It's not a question of being "religious," although that is the means many choose to explore spirituality. Rather this is an existential issue that must be decided by each individual. As aging and illness remove the ability to depend totally on the self for meeting needs, there is an inherent desire to discover or strengthen that quality of self that is impervious to fleshly decline. Connecting with the spirit and spirituality as the spirit expression is that all-important quality so often ignored by caregivers and therapists.

Many professionals fear that a search for spiritual awareness is promoting a certain religious belief, mainly that of the group leader. Just because there is no values-free counseling does not mean religious or spiritual issues can be ignored. Grimm (1994) suggested that therapists who understand their own spiritual beliefs, respect cross-cultural differences, and remain sensitive to others are capable of dealing with a client's spiritual issues in a manner that enhances the opportunity for a positive therapeutic result. Prest and Keller (1993) challenged therapists to work with those spiritual systems of clients that provide strength and support. They further contended that the decision not to deal with spirituality often begins with therapists who fail to make a distinction between spirituality and organized religion and who assume that spiritual practices are a problem rather than a positive influence in the client's life. Maher (2006) advises the use of "spiritual self-reflection" to reveal the counselor's [or leader's] attitudes about spirituality, identify any tendencies to impose the leader's beliefs on others, and awareness of ethical problems that could occur if spirituality of members is not properly respected in group.

Spirituality and Coping

Elders have a strong need to clarify their own spirituality as a coping mechanism. Options for change may be minimal in the physical or mental realm. Finding or renewing a spiritual connection can be the remaining viable change that makes the latter days of life more satisfying. This search may involve a reconnection to the past or taking a new direction to find answers in the present.

Why do therapists and group leaders find excuses to ignore spiritual, basically existential, concerns among elders? Whose mortality issues are threatened in this exploration: those of the leader or those of the elders? Working with elder groups, leaders must face the fact that death will invade and reduce the group more unpredictably than any other factor. Can you as group leader cope with so much loss? Are you knowledgeable in techniques for dealing with grief and loss issues? Two of the least effective ways to deal with this (that have been observed in other programs) is to pause for a minute of silent prayer, then move on to the regular agenda, or to ignore the event. Both approaches produce anger and distrust in elders. As a 92-year-old woman observed, "There was plenty of concern when a nurse died in a car accident, but when one of us drops, so what? Change the sheets and move in the next person as if nothing important happened." When death is downplayed, older adults feel devalued.

Each time a group member dies, the group's agenda turns to a single-session grief process. A wealth of information and training in grief groups is available through Hospice. Otherwise, a geriatric group leader prepares for this task best by seeking training or coleadership experiences to learn appropriate skills for grief groups. Hughes (1995) suggested that leaders learn to balance their psychodynamic skills with the equally important subjective skills of compassion, flexibility, listening, willingness to learn, creativity, and fallibility. Also, note that grief group exercises are given within this chapter. Other GSE activities adaptable for grief are Postcards from Eternity, in which members compose postcards to the deceased member and give wishes for a happy afterlife, and Spiritual Legacy, in which group members recall how the deceased member impressed each surviving member in ways that become lasting spiritual remembrances. An expression of spirituality, individual and sincere, is significant in coping with grief and losses that are part of aging (Reed, 1991).

Spirituality and Therapy

A group leader needs to be competent and self-aware in order to deal with each member's spirituality in a nonjudgmental, accepting manner. In spirituality, there is a wealth of metaphors useful for relaxation and introspection. Parables, stories of personal spiritual experiences, and reading the Bible, Torah, or books sacred to other religions support verbal expressions of beliefs. There are also nonverbal expressions that communicate a belief, such as a making the sign of the cross, bowing at a given time for call to prayer, or raising hands in praise. In addition, ascribing value to religious objects such as prayer books, rosary beads, or prayer shawls are nonverbal means of identifying with a formal spiritual belief system. GSE's group on spiritual symbols allows members to share these verbal and non-verbal symbols as a way in which each individual nurtures the spirit for coping.

The group leader has to clearly explain the essential variation on the Golden Rule in allowing expressions of spirituality: Respect the beliefs of others as you want them to respect your beliefs. Kept within that context, any verbal or non-verbal expressions are both healthy and informative. Recognize that some group exercises might be inappropriate for people of certain religions or beliefs who are not comfortable sharing their beliefs for whatever reason.

Another important task of the group leader is to listen attentively for clues on how to help group members recognize new possibilities for coping within their belief systems (Prest & Keller, 1993). By understanding how the individual's life is influenced by his or her belief system, the leader gets a clue as to whether the system supports or offers alternatives to presenting problems. For some elders, spirituality is associated with strongly expressed emotions while others are less de-monstrative. As McFadden (2007) noted, emotionality may or may not be linked to what McFadden and Lunsman (2009) describe as "spiritual connectedness."

If the leader feels that the elder is using spiritual beliefs to sustain negative thinking or isolating behaviors, then another approach outside group is preferred. Avoid challenging the validity of an elder's spirituality either within group or in an individual session. Make every effort to bring in a pastor, rabbi, priest, shaman, medicine man, or minister who represents the elder's belief system. Working as a team, the elder, the group leader, and the spiritual advisor hear the concerns of both client and leader. After making the connection and demonstrating positive regard, the leader disengages from the session and leaves the elder and the spiritual advisor to deal with the spiritual issues. In this way, the leader acknowledges the importance of the elder's beliefs without attempting to confuse roles by playing the part of both therapist and spiritual advisor. This is a sound approach even if the therapist is trained in theology or shares the same spiritual beliefs as the elder. Dual relationships exist in many places that are not apparent at first glance. Beware—this is one of them!

Importance of Rituals

Incorporating rituals within the GSE groups is another important element in reflection and adaptation to the later stages of life. Reminiscing or reenacting significant rituals serves as a link between the concrete and the symbolic (Cole, 1990). Sherman and Weiner (2011) built their "Transitional Keys" rituals on the work of Myerhoff (1992) to design rituals suited for the mobility, cognitive functioning, and other limitations of older adults. Familiar social and religious rituals honor, affirm, or validate an experience. Informal rituals exist in activities of daily living: for example, a preferred order of putting on clothing organizes tasks in a way that is individually satisfying. Whether formal or informal, Moore and Myerhoff (1977) defined the four elements of ritual as: "repetitive and symbolic actions, patterned behaviors, religious or secular contexts and ceremonial or everyday aspects." If even a simple ritual or system reduces anxiety and increases likelihood of task completion, then complex, symbolic, or religious rituals may go a step beyond to reduce existential anxiety.

Spirituality Groups

Spirituality: Rituals of Passage

Goals: Marking changes of time in a positive way improves self-esteem.

Process: On the marker board, write a list of familiar rituals such as confirmation, quinceanera, bar or bat mitzvah, marriage, graduation, pilgrimages, and retirement party. If possible, show pictures of the rituals important to various cultural groups. The leader initiates discussion of what is similar and different about each ritual. If not already mentioned, the leader comments on rituals as being symbolic of change. In life changes, rituals of passage mark an achievement that earns elevation to a new status. On the marker board, the leader places these rituals in order according to what the group suggests is the approximate time these occur. The leader asks open-ended questions, such as: Which of these rituals was most important to you? Was there anything about the ritual that was special? Were the sights, sounds, dress, setting, or other sensory elements important to the ritual? If you could relive one ritual of passage, which would it be?

Outcomes: Rituals of passage are important in every culture as outward symbols of life change. Reflecting on those times and the resulting changes can be very satisfying because the individual involved is usually showered with attention and goodwill. This modality recalls, re-creates, or creates ceremonies that provide social and familial connections, merging of self with beliefs, and formalizing connections with others.

Equipment list: Marker board. Photos of rituals of passage from different cultural/religious traditions.

Spirituality: Rituals of Welcome

Goals: Elders create rituals of welcome into senior years.

Process: This is an excellent follow-up to discussion on rituals of passage that is most effectively accomplished by a higher-functioning, cohesive group. The leader asks the group to recall what event or occurrence marked their entry into senior adulthood and when it happened. Was this passage marked by getting a Social Security check, registering for Medicare, retiring from work, or being eligible for senior discount cards at the pharmacy? The leader invites the group to create a ritual of welcome into senior adulthood or to congregate living (if held in a facility). This project usually takes several sessions to plan, prepare, and perform. Group members are asked what talents each might contribute to the ritual, such as singing, speaking, greeting, or arranging the program. As much as possible, the leader needs to step aside and empower the group to take control of the ritual. The leader continually poses questions, takes notes, keeps a reminder list, and coordinates resources. For example, if the group wants a formal candlelight ceremony, the leader calls a local church to borrow choir robes and candle stands. If the group decides to invite family or friends, the leader negotiates with the facility for space and time as well as volunteers to address invitations. With the group's permission, the leader takes photos or a video recording as a lasting memory that can be shared at a future session. The ritual of welcome may range from a half hour to an hour. Most facilities will allow (and even sponsor) a reception afterward. The group may agree to have the leader transcribe or script their ritual of welcome, which can become a facility tradition in welcoming newcomers quarterly or semiannually.

Outcomes: Welcome rituals for elders in their community or nursing home allow them to do what is not currently done, that is, reframe the lifestyle changes from being an albatross to an adventure with a positive beginning. The more the group takes ownership of the ritual of welcome, the more they benefit from the result. Too often elders are taken to events and not given the opportunity to be involved in the event's creation. Given artistic freedom, the rituals will take on the personality of the group: sometimes festive and sometimes serious, but always meaningful to its creative force.

Equipment list: Marker board. Other items as requested by the group.

Spirituality: Life-Changing Moments

Goals: Reflecting on events that radically changed an individual's life is a way to review the roads not taken.

Process: The leader may begin by reading Robert Frost's poem "The Road Not Taken." In this poem, a critical decision was reached and a life-changing choice was made. Inform group members that you will read the poem slowly a second time. While you are reading, each member is to try to recall an important choice that resulted in a major life change. Draw a line symbolizing a road with a fork to indicate two paths. As each member shares a personal story, create visual impact by writing a brief description of each of the paths. Seeing the words connected with the choices is a strong image. Allow members to discuss both positive and negative choices. Direct the attention of lower-functioning groups toward recalling decisions that involved positive choices and satisfactory results.

Outcomes: Choices made and chances missed are increasingly important to elders who feel that they have no opportunity to compensate for mistakes. Listen to these concerns, and give a forum for questioning false beliefs or affirming the difficult choices.

Equipment list: Robert Frost's poem "The Road Not Taken." Marker board.

Spirituality: Postcards from Eternity

Goals: Group members contemplate existence beyond this life.

Process: The leader brings in several vacation postcards with the typical "having a great time, wish you were here" message written on them. Then each member is given blank postcards on which to write a note from the future to a special person. The future place is whatever or wherever each individual believes that his or her spirit will reside after death. Everyone is free to express personal religious or philosophical views. The message needs to be short and directed to the person to whom it is addressed. If the group is hesitant to begin writing, take time to discuss various members' ideas and concerns.

Outcomes: Persons who are satisfied with their views of existence after death generally write positive comments and encouragement of advice for loved ones on how to join them. Discomfort with death and lack of spiritual resolution is evident from postcards with negative, angry messages or refusal to participate. Extreme reactions indicate the need for individual counseling on resolving life issues or pastoral counseling by the person's spiritual advisor.

Equipment list: Oversized postcards and markers.

Spirituality: Spiritual Companions

Goals: The focus is on spiritual companions as symbolic of protection for humans.

Process: Various cultures have an image of spiritual companions that appear in stories and religious folklore such as angels, ancestors, mythological characters, or saints. The leader introduces the topic by asking each member to share his or her perception of spiritual companions and whether this is an important element of their spiritual belief system. Display some pictures, dolls, or other representations of positive spiritual companions. Are spiritual companions former humans or different types of beings? What is the function of a spiritual companion? Are there special people from your past or present who seemed to show up at just the right moment to offer help? Can you be a comfort or encouragement to someone?

Outcomes: Beliefs about positive spiritual forces are another means of coping with infirmity and loneliness. Sharing those beliefs is meant to verbalize and affirm an individual's beliefs and discover that they may be shared by others.

Equipment list: Pictures, statuettes, tree decorations, dolls, or other representations of spiritual companions such as angels, mythological characters, saints, or ancestors.

Spirituality: Unseen Comforts

Goals: Using visualization, group members identify the unseen comforts that help them cope with difficulty.

Process: For this activity, the leader must be appropriately qualified and trained in visualization. The group is given a preview of what will take place during the personal journey. With whatever approach the leader is skilled in, begin the relaxation and exploration. The intent is for members to identify several difficult times in their lives, yet keep the focus on who or what was the unseen comfort that helped them in a time of problems. Keep attention on the comforting presence. Is the unseen comforter the same in several situations or different? Does the comforter have a name? Is it a living person or a spiritual being? Is that unseen comfort at a time of need? Teach a basic relaxation strategy before the close of the session.

Outcomes: Visualization is a way to unlock coping skills that seem beyond present abilities. Each person's experience is unique and need not be shared with the group. At the close of each session, members are requested to share how they presently feel on the basis of what they experienced or learned during the exercise.

Equipment list: Instrumental recording with pacing suitable for visualization. Player for the recording.

Spirituality: Spiritual Legacy

Goals: Group members consider how continuity across generations in their lives is related to the transmission of values and spirituality.

Process: The leader introduces the concept of legacy or reads a brief work on legacy. Using a four-generation genogram form (in the form of a large poster or drawn on a marker board), the leader explains the form as group members follow along on preprinted pages. The four generations are labeled as grandparents, parents, identified person with his or her generation, and children. This spiritual genogram is not as detailed as typical genograms. Giving dates, ages, and every name are not important. The spiritual genogram is completed by writing the names of family members from each generation who were most influential in teaching, changing, or establishing spiritual or religious beliefs for the identified person. To get the most from this project, the leader may direct the group in working on one generation per session. Ask group members to talk about a person within a given generation whom they thought was spiritual and why. How did that person share spirituality with others? Were there any conflicts evident between spoken beliefs and actions? Did they accept or reject that person's spiritual views? What spiritual concepts did they transmit to their children? Do their children practice what they taught or something different? How did they feel about that? Beside each significant name on the spiritual genogram, write a comment or a plus or a minus sign to indicate a positive or negative contribution to developing the present understanding of spirituality. Draw genogram lines to indicate broken, strained, or close relationships with spiritual mentors and the identified person.

Outcomes: Higher-functioning groups can resolve many unspoken issues from their lives with this critical look at spiritual values. As typical with genograms, family patterns and relationships become evident in ways formerly not acknowledged.

Equipment list: Spiritual genogram pages, marker board and boldly colored markers, or overhead projector.

Spirituality: Spiritual Symbols

Goals: Exploration of the outward signs that describe or represent spirituality.

Process: The leader poses the questions of how spirituality is shown in nonverbal ways with symbols. Show photos of spiritual symbols from various faiths such as crosses, fish, prayer beads, Star of David, and candles. After viewing the photos, the group responds by sharing what beliefs they associate with each symbol. The leader can note responses on the marker board. Is a symbol enough to fully identify a belief? Can symbols stand for more than one belief? The symbolism of candles and light has many meanings; what does it mean to each group member? What are some other symbols or nonverbal signs that are part of spiritual beliefs? Why are visual symbols used to signify an unseen concept like spirituality?

Outcomes: Elders generally cling to tradition and the outward signs of those beliefs. This discussion gives thought to how a person uses spiritual symbols and what they may communicate to others. What may also be found here is how much external symbols relate to an external locus of control compared with persons of intense internal spirituality who rely less on symbols to express spirituality.

Equipment list: Marker board and boldly colored markers. Photos of various types of religious symbols or artifacts.

Spirituality: Morality and Reality

Goals: Dealing with the death of a new or less-involved group member.

Process: Before group, the leader obtains as much information as possible (within confidentiality limits) about the group member's death. The questions most often asked by groups are these: Did she or he die peacefully? In his or her own room or at the hospital? Were any family members or friends in attendance? What are the arrangements for a funeral or memorial? At the beginning of the group, the leader announces a change in plans for today in order to honor the deceased group member. After giving basic information about the circumstances of the death and any known memorial arrangements, the leader invites questions. Without excess details or allowing a round of deathbed stories to surface, the leader asks the group to join in saying something positive about the deceased person. Comments often take this form: "I didn't know him well and I wish I had had more time to talk to him"; or "Even though he was new to our group, he had such a happy laugh that it made me laugh just to hear him." Each person may speak or choose to pass. The leader closes with a final positive comment about the deceased person. To bring the focus from mortality back to reality, the leader encourages each person to turn to the person on his or her right (and so on around the group) and say something positive or complimentary.

Outcomes: The death of any group member must be acknowledged in a respectful way. When the deceased was not well known or popular, others may feel guilty about their lack of connection to this person. Sharing positive comments about the deceased and about each other affirms them all.

Equipment list: None.

Spirituality: It's Hard to Say Goodbye

Goals: Finding a way to cope with the death of a popular, active group member.

Process: As explained in the "Morality and Reality" exercise, the leader brings information to the group in announcing the death. Bring plenty of tissues because when the deceased person was highly regarded by the group, tears may flow freely. The leader suggests that today's group be a special kind of memorial. An empty chair, representing the missing member, is placed in the center of the group. Each member takes a turn saying the farewell that they never had the opportunity to say. Some touching farewells from GSE groups have included "Dance till dawn everyday until I get there to join you"; and "Good wind with smooth sailing," followed by a military salute from a fellow veteran. As a symbol of the enduring memory of the deceased, the leader brings the empty chair back into the circle, explaining that the friendship and joy of knowing this person remains with the group always. Then, following the leader's example, each person recalls a brief story or tells what they considered special about the deceased.

Outcomes: Acknowledging the loss of a member who was special to the group needs to be done in a way that allows adequate expression of tribute in a personal way by all members. At the passing of a man whose wife was a frequent, cheerful visitor to the facility, group members asked the GSE leader to transcribe their farewell messages and present them to the widow as a token of their sympathy.

Another memorable farewell was for a 90-year-old woman who had had a quick wit. Group members felt it only fitting to share a final laugh with her by recalling her favorite jokes as a part of their memorial to her.

Equipment list: None.

Spirituality: Spiritual Connection to Holiday Traditions from Around the World

Developed with Kelly Erwin.

Goals: With the ever-growing shift in society to a more multicultural perspective, older adults are being exposed to a wider global perspective. This activity allows for armchair travel to experience the holidays from a different cultural experience.

Process: Before group, the leader should go to the local library and research how holidays are celebrated around the world. If possible, survey group members for their cultural history. Using that information, gather pictures and other visual aids to show how Chanukah, Kwanza, and Eid are celebrated in different cultures. If possible, with the facility's permission, celebrate each holiday. Encourage members to discuss the similarities and differences in how they personally celebrate during the holiday season.

Outcomes: This exercise allows members to reminisce about their personal holiday experience and fondly remember times spent with families or loved ones.

Equipment list: Pictures, music, various items needed to celebrate each holiday. Camera to capture moments by group to be shared at a later date.

Spirituality: Spiritual Legacy Time Line

Developed with Kelly Erwin.

Goals: To realize significant spiritual moments that have happened in each elder's life and the legacy they will leave for their children, grandchildren, and possible great-grandchildren.

Process: The group leader distributes a large plain piece of paper with three lines drawn horizontally and equally spaced on it. Each elder draws hash marks representing each decade of life on the top line. Below each decade, they will write down two–three spiritual milestones for each decade of life. These milestones can range from: the first memory of going to church, first communion, baptism, bar/bat mitzvah, rite of passage, sensing their own mortality, or a moment when the impossible became possible.

The second line is to briefly state the life lesson gained from each situation.

The third line identifies the person/s for whom that spiritual milestone is shared as a legacy. As they reflect on their life and the lives of their children, grandchildren, and great-grandchildren, the group leader initiates discussion on the gift they can give by sharing the stories of these spiritual milestones with their family.

Outcomes: Elders are able to reminisce and take inventory of events that they can leave as a legacy for the next generation. This might be a time of reflection and is best for higher-functioning groups.

Equipment list: Large (possible poster board size) papers. Markers or colored pencils. Tissues. Soothing music to be played in the background.

Sacred Spaces

Older adults in long term care as well as those in the community who have limited access to transportation are not able to participate with their church, synagogue, or other place of worship. Being separated from the place they consider a "sacred space" leaves a void in their spiritual connectedness. A way to that sacred space to the group is with the labyrinth. This ancient path is found today in churches, hospitals, colleges, community parks, and prisons as a way to engage individual spirituality leading to tranquility, reduction in stress, and lowering of agitation (Schultz & Rhodes, 2011). Carnes's (2001) research with Alzheimer's residents in long term care found that walking the labyrinth resulted in "short-term calming, relaxation and relief from agitation and anxiety. . . . The restorative and calming value of the walk can last from two to three hours or longer" (p. 42).

The Labyrinth Path was part of many Catholic churches in Europe. Of those that remain, the 12th century-Labyrinth at Chartres Cathedral in Paris, France, is an exceptional example of this ancient spiritual exercise built around sacred geometry. The Labyrinth Society (www.labyrinthsociety.org) and Veriditas (www. veriditas.org) are leading sources of information and scholarly research. The classic labyrinth is a circle with an entry/exit at the lower area. A walker follows the path around and finally to the center for meditation, then continues the path to the exit. Traditional classical music or other instrumental music may play in the background as the walkers move and pass each other as they follow the path.

For older adults who are not able to walk the path or if there is no labyrinth available, an alternative is the finger labyrinth. This handheld replica of the traditional labyrinth may have grooves to represent the path. A finger moves along the path in the same way that a walker would on a life-size labyrinth. The finger labyrinths are made of wood, pottery, or printed on canvas. Another option is to copy the labyrinth design and laminate the paper for finger walking.

Even without the walking experience, the use of finger labyrinths has been found effective for "relaxation and brain synchrony, which can result in more rapid establishment of trust" (Harris, 2002). The labyrinth does not come with a stated religious orientation; that is left to the personal experience of each participant. For that reason, the labyrinth (walking or finger board) is a simple way to create a sacred space for older adult groups.

Sacred Space Groups

Sacred Spaces: Walking the Labyrinth

Goals: Experience tranquility and connection with a spiritual source during meditative walks.

Process: Locate a labyrinth. Start by entering nearby area in the online Labyrinth Locator (www.labyrinthlocator.com). Devote one group session to explaining the history of the labyrinth and watching a video of the experience. On the day of the Labryinth Walk at the location, begin group with the usual welcome, then follow directions of the guide (or the leader serves as guide) to show members how to begin the walk. Arrange for chairs or benches for group members to sit before and after the walk. When all are finished, have a closing group time, inviting members to share what the walk meant to them.

Outcomes: Each person's experience will differ; however, the intent for the overall experience is a reaffirmation of personal spirituality, peaceful reflection, and increased well-being.

Equipment list: Audio recording with appropriate speakers featuring calm, classical music. Find a walking path labyrinth locally at a church, park, hospital, college, or other location. If this is not possible, secure permission to set up a smaller version of a labyrinth in an indoor or outdoor space. Indoor paths could be marked with removable colored tape. Outdoor paths could be marked with small cones. Exact precision may not be feasible, but the concept can still be meaningful. For cognitively impaired elders, ask permission from the long term care facility to set up a small labyrinth within an enclosed garden area where patients with dementia can move around safely. Creating a labyrinth is an excellent creative task for an Eagle Scout troop that seeks community service projects or a family support group. Example of a labyrinth for Alzheimer's residents is at Alexian Brothers Valley Residence in Chattanooga, Tennessee.

Sacred Spaces: Finger Labyrinth

Goals: Experience tranquility and connection with a spiritual source during meditative movement.

Process: For ease of use, provide a laminated paper version of finger labyrinths for each group member or for pairs of two unless possible to have several wood or ceramic grooved labyrinths.

Start and finish the same as for the walking labyrinth.

Outcomes: As with walking, the finger tracing experience will differ; however, the intent for the overall experience is a reaffirmation of personal spirituality, peaceful reflection, and increased well-being. If group members work as a team with one labyrinth, this adds an element of connection in the sharing.

For cognitively impaired elders, the finger labyrinth can be easier to manage. Do not bring this group to an open outdoor location without adequate supervision as persons with dementia can wander away or feel confused and frustrated by the winding paths. Finger labyrinths may be the better option for this group.

Equipment list: Finger labyrinth on laminated paper or wood/ceramic grooved labyrinth. Audio recording with appropriate speakers featuring calm, classical music.

Sacred Spaces: Meditation Garden

Goals: Incorporate the sensory inputs of nature with meditation to enhance the spiritual experience.

Process: Bring the group to an outdoor garden, either at the facility/community center or nearby location. If at a public garden, choose a time of day when the garden is not crowded. The leader has a plan arranged for three stops within the garden to meditate. At the first stop, the leader reads a small passage about the beauty of nature and asks the group to think/pray/meditate on what is seen around them. At the second stop, the leader asks group members to listen to sounds in the garden, asking members to say what they hear (i.e., birds, ducks, mosquitoes buzzing, wind, etc). At the third stop, the leader reads another passage about the beauty of nature and invites members to share a feeling or thought about being in this place at this time. An alternative is to ask, "If you chose a flower or plant as a symbol of your life and accomplishments, which would you choose?"

Outcomes: Surrounded by a lush garden brings a sense of calm and reminder of beauty that is in nature. By focusing outward to nature and meditating/praying/thinking about the here and now, group members see that present limitations do not erase the joy of being in a garden, reflecting on self and spirituality.

Equipment list: If there is not a garden at the facility or community center, locate a nearby garden to visit. Bring a digital camera and offer to take a photo of each group member with the flower/plant that he or she chose as a life symbol. After the photos are printed, the leader gives a photo to each member with a personal note of thanks for participation.

Sacred Spaces: Water Feature

Goals: Finding calm from the sounds of water at a fountain brings peace and stimulates memories. Water is necessary for sustaining life and is also a spiritual symbol associated with various religious practices.

Process: Find a water fountain in the garden of a facility or community center. If none is available, bring in a tabletop water fountain with flowing water. Invite group members to listen to the sound of the water and give the first thought that comes to mind. Or ask group members to recall a time when water was part of spiritual expression and describe the event. The group leader asks members to give a word that is associated with water, for example, water = life, water = cleanliness, water = refreshment. Write each word on the marker board. Invite group members to add a spiritual word association with water such as baptism, purity, cleansing, ritual, or reviving. Water is also one of the four life elements: earth, air, fire, and water.

Outcomes: The sound of water stimulates memories of spiritual associations with water. Some associations will be specifically religious, while others are generalized. Each group member expresses something about his/her beliefs of life in sharing the meaning of water. Beliefs shared are beliefs affirmed, which is part of the value of this modality.

Equipment list: Find a nearby water fountain or tabletop water fountain that has moving water (can be purchased for $10–20 dollars at retail stores or a garden shop).

Sacred Spaces: Shoebox Altars

Developed with Lynn Ellyn Robinson, MSCP.

Goals: Construct and prepare a "sacred space" (altar) that is portable and supports the participants in focusing on the deepening of spiritual life, as well as connecting to their own spiritual expression.

Process: The leader begins by asking group members to describe their experiences of what traditional altars look like and the value of altars as related to their spiritual life. The leader will make a list of descriptors participants provide and, if necessary, add some to fill out the list. The leader makes another list as members name specific altar elements that have been significant in their spiritual development. The leader encourages participants to state a word that represents an aspect of spirituality that they find most comforting (for example, joy, peace, compassion, generosity, etc.), then write that word on a smooth stone or card (provided). The word can become the main theme of the altar that each group member constructs inside the shoe box, including inside and outside of the box and the lid. The design is intended to be arranged so that each box is placed on its side, and the altar sits inside the lid for display. Small objects can be added or images/words from magazines. Family photos may be added if available. These personal, constructed altars can be added to over time.

Outcomes: Participants have the experience of creating their own (portable) place of worship or meditation that incorporates a focus of their choice. For higher-functioning elders, this gives a way to enhance their cognitive acuity and the taking of responsibility for their spiritual lives. Lower-functioning groups or those with less digital dexterity need assistance from the leader and volunteers to construct their altars. The shoebox altar is portable and can be displayed or kept private. For older adults in long term care or assisted living who miss the opportunity to attend a service at their preferred place of worship, this small sacred space can fill a large void in their spiritual expression.

Equipment list: Marker board and appropriate markers, shoe boxes, colored papers, adhesives (glue sticks, tape, etc.), brightly colored permanent markers, battery-operated votive candles, smooth stones or index cards that have been cut in half (to write the focus word upon), fabric and lace scraps, magazines (from which to glean pictures), small silk flowers, colored beads, and other found items that could be incorporated into an altar.

10

THE FUTURE OF GERIATRIC GROUPS WITH NEW ELDER GENERATION

As the Baby Boomers slide into the older adult ranks, the concepts of geriatric group work are expanding to serve an older population that includes dramatically different cohort experiences. At the same time, the oldest-old are living longer. For the geriatric group leader, this increases the challenges to choose and implement a program that spans these generational distinctions. Preparing for the future requires attention to the following 10 Targets for the Next Generation of Geriatric Group Work.

Ten Targets for the Next Generation of Geriatric Group Work

Target 1: Teaching Gerontology as a Core Course

The dramatic growth of the aging population means that every psychologist/counselor/social worker needs training in aging and geriatric issues. Zucchero (1998) found that this training is not a core course for licensed professionals in clinical psychology and counseling, and little has changed going forward into a second decade. The 2001 Council for Accreditation of Counseling and Related Educational Programs (CACREP) Standards are consistent with the "area of concentration model" (Stickle & Onedera, 2006). The 2009 CACREP standards dropped specifics for gerontology coursework at a time when this subject is both needed and increasingly in demand.

Gerontology does not fit in a tidy box. Gerontology encompasses adult development, career, role exit, marriage and family, addiction, health, nutrition, dementia and cognitive impairments, death and dying, as well as medical and psychological disorders. To view an individual not as an old person but rather a whole person is consistent with the Inter-Disciplinary Model (Stickle & Onedera,

2006). At the least, professionals in mental health and psychology need at least a core course in gerontology and aging issues to be appropriately prepared for practice in the 2000s and beyond.

Target 2: Integration with Managed Care or National Health Care

Managed care may continue in the private sector or become absorbed into a yet unknown national health care system, which leaves geriatric care services competing with other care needs for support. Fortunately, managed care systems are generally favorable to group programs as cost-efficient options to individual counseling services. However, with the political and financial pressures on health care, changes in reimbursement or denial of services can occur with minimal warning. If a different system of national health care becomes the standard, there is no way to predict acceptance of group therapy within a long term care setting.

Presently, what can be done? Don't request authorization for group services and assume that approval follows. With each request or initial contracting, send a concise package of how the group program, goals, and outcomes justify approval. To make a positive impression, present a sample group schedule, qualifications of the leaders, and letters or comments from the facility administrator, nursing supervisor, or physicians who attest to the therapeutic value of the group program.

Target 3: Multicultural Awareness

Whether groups are conducted in a therapeutic setting, assisted living, or community center, group leaders need training in multicultural sensitivity and communication. America no longer fits the old description of a melting pot, but rather a banquet enriched by many races and cultures. Group leaders are challenged to understand the cultural influences, social norms, and gestures of respect that are appropriate for an increasingly multicultural elder population.

University sociology departments and local government urban planning agencies can provide updated information on the local demographics represented in the geographic area served by a geriatric group program. Nurses, psychologists, and licensed psychotherapists generally have training in multicultural issues. Students and volunteers need to have basic training in multicultural awareness, particularly regarding the ethnicities and cultures represented in the geriatric group program.

Target 4: Greater Emphasis on Assessment

All group leaders need to establish standards for intake, assessment, evaluation, and follow-up that are suitable to each type of group. Nurses, psychologists, and licensed psychotherapists are qualified for a wider range of assessment tools. When the groups are reimbursed as treatment, the professional level standards of care must be followed. For groups in the community or those not reimbursed as therapy, a reasonable type of entry assessment needs to be followed. When possible, group leaders are wise to obtain approval or referral into group from physicians or facility staff.

Target 5: Improving Norms and Standards for Older Adult Assessments

In choosing an assessment for professional use, attention must be given to updated norms, preferably with defined age categories (for example, the age 60–69 young-old is a notably different group than the overage 80 oldest-old). Some instruments are long overdue for updating. Another concern for professionals is choosing assessments appropriate for a multicultural elder population. Here is an area that cries out for new and better assessment options with relevant age cohort norms.

Target 6: Programs for Homeless Elders

Socially isolated homeless elders remain an underserved population. Opportunities to serve these elders may be largely volunteer driven with groups as part of an urban community center, food bank, or faith-based organization. With longer life comes the risk of outliving resources, complicated by economic downturn. An increasing number of older adults who once enjoyed a middle class lifestyle have become part of the new poor or homeless.

Based on population estimates from the U.S. Department of Housing and Urban Development, the number of homeless older adults is expected to increase by 38% between 2010 and 2020 with the potential to double by 2050 (Sermons & Henry, 2010). Factors in homelessness for other adults are economic, widowhood, lack of family support, and chronic mental illness—all of which are complicated by confusion and distrust of the social services system with which newly homeless elders have little experience. Group programs at a community or faith-based organization can be a way to show acceptance and help these isolated elders connect with others who are in a similar situation. Group leaders also need to be knowledgeable about food banks, social programs, free medical clinics, county medical services, and any useful resource that can demonstrate to the homeless elder that someone cares. At the same time, there is a lack of research on the psychosocial needs of homeless elders. University sociology, nursing, psychology, or counseling departments can bring in students under professional supervision to provide free geriatric groups that will benefit the elders and provide research opportunities to better understand how to serve those needs.

Target 7: Relationship Issues of Elder Couples

As men and women live longer past traditional retirement at age 65, they have the same concerns as other adults in efforts to sustain or develop romantic relationships. The older adult couple's adjustment to the empty nest and spending more time together after retirement is being interrupted by a new phenomenon: the boomerang adult child. Not only are adult children returning home after job loss, divorce, substance abuse, or domestic violence, but often they come with grandchildren, turning the retirement haven into a multigenerational household.

The golden anniversary celebrations are fewer than in a generation past as elder couples are being torn apart by divorce, addictions, or domestic violence. At older ages, women continue to outnumber men, which can lead to a dating scene as competitive as a trendy young adult club. Dating and mating can be more popular than the afternoon bridge game for single seniors who seek a new romantic relationship. Group leaders who work with community dwelling elders can expect to deal with issues of attraction, sexuality, breakups, and commitments within the group and as part of the discussions.

Target 8: Training in Elder Abuse and Domestic Violence

Physical, emotional, and sexual abuse may be the modern-day equivalent of bubonic plague in the devastation that is left behind for individuals and their families. Sadly, abuse of older adults has become so rampant that states have specific laws for mandatory reports of elder abuse.

All geriatric group leaders, regardless of professional or student/volunteer status, need regular training in recognizing the signs of domestic violence, neglect, manipulation, and intimidation of elders. Perpetrators of elder abuse include spouses, adult children, relatives, financial managers, and caregivers. Elder abuse can occur in private homes, assisted living, nursing homes, rehabilitation centers, and hospitals. Never assume that an elder living alone or with relatives is more or less at risk that one living in long term care.

Group leaders need to know the state statutory definition of who is a mandatory reporter for suspected elder abuse. Here are important questions: Can a report be made by a telephone hotline, or must it be in writing? Does every group leader know the procedure for reporting and how to document this action in the group program records? Group leaders need to be prepared to help suspected elder abuse victims contact the local domestic violence shelter, crisis intake center, social service agency with local jurisdiction, or area nursing home ombudsman office.

Target 9: Counseling Readiness of 21st-Century Elders

The Baby Boomer generation enters older adulthood with a different view of counseling or group participation than that of their parents' generation. These newest elders who came from the 1960s era of communal living and encounter groups generally view counseling as an acceptable option for dealing with personal, relationship, or family problems. They have a history of being outspoken and seeking self-improvement. Among this group are those who have participated in support groups, substance abuse groups, and personal growth groups. As a result, geriatric group leaders who work with a Baby Boomer population are likely to spend less time in the formative stages of the group with potential for more intense and productive working group interactions. Because many of these new elders are group savvy, they have more preconceived ideas of how groups function and what constitutes an effective leader.

Target 10: Opportunities for the Practitioner-Researcher

Geriatric group work occurs in the field, not the lab. Bringing services to the assisted care, nursing home, or community center where elders live or congregate is beneficial to them and increases the consistency of group attendance. What a dissertation-frantic doctoral student may see as a "convenience sample" is actually a gift for research, working with elders in their environment where they feel more comfortable.

Think beyond thesis, dissertation, and publish-or-perish expectations. This is a developing model for group work with a growing population in which much is yet to be learned. Share discoveries, ideas, and theories with other practitioners. Become interdisciplinary, and get outside your own field to connect with other geriatric group leaders in nursing, social work, psychology, psychotherapy, activity directors, and community center directors. Don't be satisfied with attending geriatric conferences and soaking up information; be a presenter. Bring back what was learned from professional conferences to share with facility staff.

Listen more than speak. Listen to the elder group members talk about their wants, needs, and aspirations. Listen as carefully as to the nursing home administrator. Listen to volunteers and students who have a bud of an idea for research but may need help in working that idea into a study. Look for modalities in this book that were developed by my student research team who took my work into exciting new directions. Be mindful that too many good ideas waste away in chart notes—mine that gold. This book is the result of sharing ideas to encourage other geriatric group leaders to do more and do it better.

A Final Observation

Gerontology remains wide open for development of new approaches. Like any remaining uncharted territory, it's not as safe as another review of Freud or as predictable as riffs on rational behavior. The bookshelves on geriatric group work are not filled. What will you contribute?

Geriatric group work is waiting for the select, the capable, the creative, and the bold. Group leaders in the field are defining the future of geriatric group work daily by meeting the needs of real people. Take these ideas, improve on them, and be that leader.

REFERENCES

American Association of Therapeutic Humor (AATH). (2000). http://www.aath.org

Australian Nursing Journal. (2011). News: Laughter versus antipsychotics. *Australian Nursing Journal, 19*(4). Retrieved from www.aath.org

Berkman, L. F., Glass, T., Brissette, I., and Seeman, T. E. (2000). From social integration to health: Durkheim in the new millennium. *Social Science & Medicine, 51,* 843–857.

Bierma, J. (1998). *Remotivation group therapy: Handbook for the basic course.* Andover, MA: National Remotivation Therapy Organization, Inc.

Birren, J. (1987). The best of all stories. *Psychology Today, 21,* 91–92.

Blau, Z.S. (1973). *Old age in a changing society.* New York: New Viewpoints.

Brodaty, H., Low, L.F., Chenoweth, L., & Fleming, R. (2011). Sydney multisite intervention of Laughter Bosses and Elder Clowns (SMILE): A randomized controlled trial of humor therapy in residential care. *DCRC Assessment and Better Care.* Retrieved from http://www.dementia.unsw.edu.au/index.php?option=com_dcrc&view=dcrc&layout=project&Itemid=112&pid=47

Brummett, B.H., Barefoot, J.C., Seigler, I.C., Clapp-Channing, N.E., Lytle, B.L., Bosworth, H.B., . . . Mark, D.B. (2001). Characteristics of socially isolated patients with coronary artery disease who are at elevated risk for mortality. *Psychosomatic Medicine, 63,* 267–272.

Bryant, W. (1991). Creative group work with confused elderly people: A development of sensory integration therapy. *British Journal of Occupational Therapy, 54*(5), 187–192.

Burge, S., & Street, D. (2010). Advantage and choice: Social relationships and staff assistance in assisted living. *Journal of Gerontology: Social Sciences, 65B,* 358–369

Burlew, L.D., Jones, J., & Emerson, P. (1991). Exercise and the elderly: A group counseling approach. *The Journal for Specialist in Group Work, 16*(3), 152–158.

Burnside, I.M. (1973). *Psychosocial nursing care of the aged.* New York: McGraw Hill.

Burnside, I.M., & Schmidt, M.G. (1994). *Working with older adults: Group process and techniques* (3rd ed.). Boston: Jones & Bartlett.

Butler, R.N. (1963). The life review: An interpretation of reminiscence in the aged. *Psychiatry, 26,* 65–76.

Butler, R.N. (1975). *Why survive? Being old in America.* New York: Harper and Row.

Carnes, V.B. (2001). Walking the labyrinth to peace. Not-for-profit report. *Nursing Homes Long Term Care Management, 50*(10), 41–42.

Clark, A.J. (2004). On the meaning of color in early recollections. *The Journal of Individual Psychology, 63,* 214–224.

Clark, A.J. (2008). Early recollections and sensory modalities. *Journal of Individual Psychology, 64*(3), 353–368.

Cohen-Mansfielf, J., Parpura-Gill, A., Kotler, M., Vass, J., MacLennan, B., & Rosenberg, F. (2007). Shared Interest Groups (SHIGS) in low income independent living facilities. *Clinical Gerontologist, 31*(1), 101–112.

Cole, M. (1990). Ritual and therapy: Casting the circle of change. *Pratt Institute Creative Arts Therapy Review, 11,* 13–21.

Conwell, Y. (2001). Suicide in later life: A review and recommendations for prevention. *Suicide and Life Threatening Behavior, 31*(Suppl.), 32–47.

Corbett, B. (2007). Embedded: Nursing home undercover. *AARP The Magazine, 50*(1), 70–96.

Corey, M.C., Corey, G., & Corey, C. (2010). *Groups: Process and practice* (8th ed.). Belmont, CA: Brooks/Cole.

Cousins, N. (1979). *Anatomy of an illness as perceived by the patient.* New York: W.W. Norton.

Dalby, P. (2006). Is there a process of spiritual change or development associated with aging? A critical review of research. *Aging & Mental Health, 10*(1), 4–12.

Dewey, J. (1939). *Theory of valuation.* Chicago: University of Chicago Press.

Dimmer, S.A., Carroll, J.L., & Wyatt, G.K. (1990). Uses of humor in psychotherapy. *Psychological Reports, 66,* 795–801.

Erikson, E.H. (1950). *Childhood and society.* New York: Norton.

Erlanger, M.A. (1990). Using genograms with the older client. *Journal of Mental Health Counseling, 12*(3), 321–330.

Erwin, K. (1993). Looking backward, looking ahead: Helping elders cope. *Christian Counseling Today, 1*(3), 33–36.

Ferrucci, L., & Simonsick, E.M. (2006). A little exercise. *Journals of Gerontology Series A: Biological Sciences & Medical Sciences, 61A*(11), 1154–1156.

Floyd, M. (2003). Bibliotherapy as an adjunct to psychotherapy for depression in older adults. *Journal of Clinical Psychology, 59,* 187–195.

Folsom, J. (1968). Reality orientation for the elderly mental patient. *Journal of Geriatric Psychiatry, 1,* 291–307.

Franzini, L. (2001). Humor in therapy: The case for training therapists in its uses and risks. *The Journal of General Psychology, 128*(2), 170–193.

Glass, T.A., Mendes de Leon, C.F., Marottolie, R.A., & Berkman, L.F. (1999). Population based study of social and productive activities as predictors of survival among elderly Americans. *British Medical Journal, 319*(21), 478–483.

Glasser, W. (1965). *Reality therapy: A new approach to psychiatry.* New York: Harper & Row.

Goodyear, J., & Abraham, I.L. (1994). Effects of relaxing music on agitation during meals among nursing home residents with severe cognitive impairment. *Archives of Psychiatric Nursing, 8,* 150–158.

Grimm, D.W. (1994). Therapist spiritual and religious values in psychotherapy. *Counseling and Values, 38*(3), 154–164.

Haight, B., & Gibson, F. (2005). *Burnside's working with older adults.* Burlington, MA: Jones & Bartlett Learning.

Hanser, S.B. (1988). Controversy in music listening and stress reduction research. *Arts Psychotherapy, 15,* 211–217.

Harlan, J.E. (1993). The therapeutic value of art for persons with Alzheimer's disease and related disorders. *Loss, Grief and Care, 6,* 99–106.

Harvard Health Publications. (2009). The health benefits of Tai Chi. Retrieved from http://www.health.harvard.edu/newsletters/Harvard_Womens_Health_Watch/2009/May/The-health-benefits-of-tai-chi

Havinghurst, R.J., & Glasser, A. (1972). An exploratory study of reminiscence. *Journal of Gerontology, 27,* 245–253.

Hern, B.G., & Weis, D.M. (1991). A group counseling experience with the very old. *Journal for Specialists in Group Work, 16,* 143–151.

Hicks-Moore, S.L. (2005). Relaxing music at mealtime in nursing homes: Effects on agitated patients with dementia. *Journal of Gerontological Nursing, 31*(12), 26–32.

Hooker, K., & McAdams, D.P. (2003). Personality reconsidered: A new agenda for aging research. *Journals of Gerontology: Psychological Sciences, 58,* 296–304.

House, J.S. (2001). Social isolation kills, but how and why? *Psychosomatic Medicine, 63*(2), 273–274.

Hughes, M. (1995). *Bereavement and support; healing in a healthy group environment.* Washington, DC: Taylor & Francis.

Hyden, L.C., & Orulv, L. (2009). Narrative and identity in Alzheimer's disease: A case study. *Journal of Aging Studies, 23*(4), 205–214.

Hynes, A.M., & Wendl, L.C. (1990). Bibliotherapy: An interactive process in counseling older persons. *Journal of Mental Health Counseling, 12*(3), 288–302.

Johnson, C., Lahey, P., & Shore, A. (1992). An exploration of creative arts therapeutic group work on an Alzheimer's unit. *Arts in Psychotherapy, 19*(4), 269–277.

Johnson, C.M., & Sullivan-Marx, E.M. (2006). Art therapy: Using the creative process for healing and hope among African American older adults. *Geriatric Nursing, 27*(5), 309–316.

Kabat-Zinn, J. (2005). *Coming to our senses: Healing ourselves and the world through mindfulness.* New York: Hyperion.

Karel, M.J., Gatz, M., & Smyer, M.A. (2012). Aging and mental health in the decade ahead. *The American Psychologist, 67*(3), 184–198.

Kartman, L. (1991). Life review: One aspect of making meaningful music for the elderly. *Activities, Adaptation & Aging, 15,* 45–52.

Kohlberg, L. (1963). The development of children's orientation toward a moral order: Sequence in the development of moral thought. *Vita Humana, 6,* 11–35.

Kontos, P.C. (2005). Embodied selfhood in Alzheimer's disease. Rethinking person-center care. *Dementia, 4*(4), 553–570.

Lazarus, A. (1976). Multimodal behavior therapy. In C.M. Franks (Series Ed.), *Springer series in behavior modification: Vol. I.* New York: Springer.

Lee, K.H. (2011). The role of spiritual experience, forgiveness adn religious support on the general well-being of older adults. *Journal of Religion, Spirituality and Aging, 23*(3), 206–233.

Lewis, G.L. (1979). Adler's theory of personality and art therapy in a nursing home. *Art Psychotherapy, 6,* 47–50.

Lewis, M. (2001). Spirituality, counseling and elderly: An introduction to the spiritual life review. *Journal of Adult Development, 8*(4), 231–240.

Lewis, M., & Butler, R.N. (1974). Life review therapy: Putting memories to work in individual and group psychotherapy. *Geriatrics, 29,* 1304–1305.

Li, F., Harmer, P., Fisher, K.J., & McAuley, E. (2004). Tai Chi: Improving functional balance and predicting subsequent falls in older persons. *Medicine and Science in Sports and Exercise, 36*(12), 2046–2052.

Lindeman, D.A., Downing, R., Corby, N.H., & Sanborn, B. (1991). *Alzheimer's day care: A basic guide*. New York: Hemisphere.

LoGerfo, M. (1980–1981). Three ways of reminiscence in theory and practice. *International Journal of Aging & Human Development, 12*(1), 39–48.

Lowenthal, R.I., & Marrazzo, R.A. (1990). Milestoning: Evoking memories for resocialization through group reminiscence. *The Gerontologist, 30,* 269–272.

Maher, A. (2006). Incorporating spirituality into the therapeutic setting: Safeguarding ethical use of spirituality through therapist self-reflection. In K. Helmeke & C. Sori (Eds.), *The therapist's notebook for integrating spirituality in counseling: Homework, handouts and activities for use in psychotherapy* (pp. 19–28). Binghamton, NY: Haworth Press.

Mains, J.A., & Scogin, F.R. (2003). The effectiveness of self-administered treatments: A practice friendly review of the research. *Journal of Clinical Psychology, 59,* 237–246.

Maslow, A.H. (1959). *New knowledge in human values*. New York: Harper & Brothers.

McAdams, D.P. (2005). *The redemptive self: Stories Americans live by*. New York: Oxford Press.

McCarthy, C.J., & Hart, S. (2011). Designing groups to meet evolving challenges in health care settings. *The Journal for Specialists in Group Work, 36*(4), 352–367.

McFadden, S.H. (2007). Religion and spirituality. In J.E. Birren (Editor in Chief), *Encyclopedia of gerontology: Age, aging and the aged* (2nd ed., pp. 410–417). Oxford, England: Elsevier.

McFadden, S.H., & Lunsman, M. (2009). Arts involvement and spirituality as sources of well-being in older people. *Journal of Religion, Spirituality & Aging, 21,* 330–343.

McGuire, F.A., Boyo, R., & James, A. (1992). *Therapeutic humor with the elderly*. New York: Haworth Press.

McKinley, F. (1977). Exploration in bibliotherapy. *Personnel and Guidance Journal, 56,* 550–552.

McLean, K.C., Pasupathi, M., & Pals, J.L. (2007). Selves creating stories creating selves: A process model of self-development. *Personality and Social Psychology Review, 11,* 262–278.

McLeod, J. (1996). The emerging narrative approach to counseling and psychotherapy. *British Journal of Guidance and Counseling, 24*(2), 173–184.

McMurray, J. (1989). Creative arts with older people. *Activities, Adaptation and Aging, 14,* 1–138.

Mendes de Leon, C.F., Glass, T.A., & Berkman, L.F. (2003). Social engagement and disability in community population of older adults. The New Haven EPESE. *American Journal of Epidemiology, 157*(7), 633–642.

Merriam, S. (1989). The structure of simple reminiscence. *Gerontologist, 29*(6), 761–767.

Minardi, H., & Hayes, N. (2003). Nursing older adults with mental health problems: Therapeutic interventions part 2. *Gerontological Nursing Practice, 15*(7), 20–24.

Moore, L.A., & Davis, B. (2002). Quilting narrative: Using repetition techniques to help elderly communicators. *Geriatric Nursing, 23,* 262–266.

Moore, S.F., & Myerhoff, B.G. (1977). Secular ritual: Forms and meanings. In S.F. Moore & B.G. Myerhoff (Eds.), *Secular ritual*. Amsterdam, Netherlands: Van Gorcum.

Murphy, M.C., Conley, J., & Hernandez, M.A. (1994). Group remotivation therapy for the '90s. *Perspectives in Psychiatric Care, 30,* 9–12.

Murrock, C.J., & Higgins, P.A. (2009). The theory of music, mood and movement to improve health outcomes. *Journal of Advanced Nursing, 65*(10), 2249–2257.

Myerhoff, B. (1992). *Remembered lives: The work of ritual, storytelling and growing older*. Ann Arbor: University of Michigan Press.

National Remotivation Therapy Organization. (1995). *NRTO policy & procedure manual*. Retrieved from www.remotivation.com

Park, N.S. (2009). The relationship of social engagement to psychological well-being of older adults in assisted living facilities. *Journal of Applied Gerontology, 28,* 461–481.

Park, N.S., Zimmerman, S., Kinslow, K., Shin, H.J., & Roff, L.L. (2012). Social engagement in assisted living and implications for practice. *Journal of Applied Gerontology, 31*(1), 215–238.

Pasupathi, M., & Carstensen, L.L. (2003). Age and emotional experience during mutual reminiscing. *Psychology and Aging, 18*(3), 430–442.

Pennebaker, J.W. (1997). Writing about emotional experiences as a therapeutic process. *Psychological Science, 8*(3), 162–166.

Pennebaker, J.W. (2000). Telling stories: The health benefits of narrative. *Literature and Medicine, 19*(1), 3–18.

Pennebaker, J.W., & Beall, S.K. (1986). Confronting a traumatic event: Toward an understanding of inhibition and disease. *Journal of Abnormal Psychology, 95,* 274–281.

Pennebaker, J.W., & Seagal, J.D. (1999). Forming a story: The health benefits of narrative. *Journal of Clinical Psychology, 55*(10), 1243–1254.

Peterkin, A.D., & Perryman, A.A. (2009). Finding a voice: Revisiting the history of therapeutic writing. *Medical Humanities, 35,* 80–88.

Phillips-Silver, J. (2009). On the meaning of movement in music, development and the brain. *Contemporary Music Review, 28*(3), 293–314.

Piaget, J. (1965). The moral judgment of the child. M. Gabin (Trans.). New York: Free Press. (Original work published 1932).

Pilkington, P.D., Windsor, T.D., & Crisp, D.A. (2012). Volunteering and subjective well-being in midlife and older adults: The role of supportive social networks. *Journals of Gerontology Series B: Psychological Sciences & Social Sciences, 67B*(2), 249–260.

Prest, L.A. & Keller, J.F. (1993). Spirituality and family therapy: Spiritual beliefs, myths and metaphors. *Journal of Marital and Family Therapy, 19*(2), 137–148.

Raths, L., Hamin, M., & Simon, S. (1966). *Values and teaching: Working with values in the classroom.* Columbus, OH: Charles E. Merrill.

Reed, P.G. (1991). Spirituality and mental health in older adults: Extant knowledge for nursing. *Family and Community Health, 14*(2), 14–25.

Robinson, A.M. (n.d.). *Remotivation techniques: A manual for use in nursing homes.* Philadelphia: American Psychiatric Association/Smith, Kline & French Laboratories Remotivation Project.

Rogers, C.R. (1961). *On becoming a person.* Boston: Houghton Mifflin.

Rook, K.S. (2009). Gaps in social support resources in later life: An adaptational challenge in need of further research. *Journal of Social and Personal Relationships, 26*(1), 103–113.

Rutherford, K. (1994). Humor in psychotherapy. *Individual Psychology Journal of Alderian Theory, 50,* 207–222.

Ryff, C.D., Kwan, C.M.L., & Singer, B.H. (2001). Personality and aging: Flourishing agendas and future challenges. In J.E. Birren & K.W. Schaie (Eds.), *Handbook of the psychology of aging* (5th ed., pp. 477–499). San Diego, CA: Academic Press.

Schnarch, D.M. (1990). Therapeutic uses of humor in psychotherapy. *Journal of Family Psychotherapy, 1,* 75–86.

Schultz, E.D., & Rhodes, J.W. (2011). The labyrinth as a path of healing. Poster presentation at the American Holistic Nurses Association Annual Conference, Louisville, KY.

Scogin, F., Hamblin, D., & Beutler, L. (1987). Bibliotherapy for depressed older adults: A self-help alternative. *The Gerontologist, 27*(3), 383–387.

Scogin, F., Welsh, D., Hanson, A., Stump, J., & Coates, A. (2005). Evidence-based psychotherapies for depression in older adults. *Clinical Psychology: Science and Practice, 12,* 222–234.

Seccombe, K., & Ishii-Kuntz, M. (1991). Perceptions of problems associated with aging: Comparisons among four older age cohorts. *The Gerontologist, 31*(4), 527–533.

Sermons, M.W., & Henry, M. (2010). Demographics of homelessness series: The rising elderly population. *Homelessness Research Institute*, National Alliance to End Homelessness. Retrieved from www.endhomelessness.org/content/article/detail/2698

Shahidi, M., Mojtahed, L., Modabbernia, A., Mojtahed, M., Shafiabady, A., Delavar, Al, & Honari, H. (2011). Laughter yoga versus group exercise program in elderly depressed women: A randomized controlled trial. *International Journal of Geriatric Psychiatry, 26*(3), 333–327.

Shaw, B.A., Krause, N., Liang, J., & Bennett, J. (2007). Tracking changes in social relations throughout late life. *Journals of Gerontology Series B: Psychological Sciences & Social Sciences, 62B*(2), S90–S99.

Sherman, A., & Weiner, M. (2011). Transforming inspiration to program application: The journal of transitional keys. *Journal of the American Society on Aging, 35*(3), 37–51.

Sherman, S., & Havinghurst, R.J. (1970). An exploratory study of reminiscence. *The Gerontologist, 10,* 42.

Stickle, F., & Onedera, J.D. (2006). Teaching gerontology in counselor education. *Educational Gerontology, 32*(4), 247–259.

Street, D., & Burge, S. (2012). Residential context, social relationships and subjective well-being in assisted living. *Research on Aging, 34*(3), 365–394.

Street, D., Burge, S., Quandagno, J., & Barrett, A. (2007). The salience of social relationships for resident wellbeing in assisted living. *Journal of Gerontology, Series B: Psychological Sciences and Social Sciences, 62,* S129–S134.

Sue, D.W., & Sue, D. (1990). *Counseling the culturally different.* New York: John Wiley & Sons.

Sue, D.W., & Sue, D. (2003). *Counseling the culturally diverse: Theory and practice* (4th ed.). New York: Wiley.

Sullivan, F.R., Bird, E.D., Alpay, M., & Cha, J.J. (2001). Remotivation therapy and Huntington's disease. *Journal of Neuroscience Nursing, 33*(3), 136–142.

Swenson, A.B. (1991). Relationships: Art education, art therapy and special education. *Perceptual and Motor Skills, 12*(3), 165–169.

Tobin, S.S., & Gustafson, J.D. (1987). Work we do differently with elderly clients. *Journal of Gerontological Social Work, 10,* 107–121.

Tornstam, L. (1989). Gero-transcendence: A reformulation of the disengagement theory. *Aging, 1,* 55–63.

Toseland, R.W., & Rivas, R.F. (2005). *An introduction to group work practice* (5th ed.). Boston: Allyn and Bacon.

Toseland, R.W., & Rizzo, V.M. (2004). What's different about working with older people in groups? *Journal of Gerontological Social Work, 44*(1), 5–24.

Turesky, D.G., & Schultz, J.M. (2010). Spirituality among older adults: An exploration of the developmental context, impact on mental and physical health and integration into counseling. *Journal of Religion, Spirituality & Aging, 22,* 162–179.

Tuttman, A. (1991). On utilizing humor in group psychotherapy. *Group, 15,* 246–256.

U.S. Census Bureau. (2010). *The next four decades: The older population in the United States: 2010–2050* (pp. 25–1138). Retrieved from http://www.census.gov/prod/2010pubs/p25–1138.pdf

Voukelatos, A., Cumming, R.G., Lord, S.R., & Rissel, C. (2007). A randomized, controlled trial of Tai Chi for prevention of falls: The Central Sydney Tai Chi trial. *Journal of the American Geriatrics Society, 55*(8), 1185–1191.

Wallace, J.B. (1992). Reconsidering the life review: The social construction of talk about the past. *The Gerontologist, 32*(1), 120–125.

Watt, L.M., & Wong, P. (1991). A taxonomy of reminiscence and therapeutic implications. *Journal of Gerontological Social Work, 16,* 37–57.

Webster, J.D. (1999). World views and narrative gerontology: Situating reminiscence behavior within a lifespan perspective. *Journal of Aging Studies, 13,* 29–42.

Webster, J.D. (2001). The future of the past: Continuing challenges for reminiscence research. In G. Kenone, B. DeVries, & P. Clark (Eds.), *Narrative gerontology: Theory, research, and practice* (pp. 159–185). New York: Springer.

Webster, J. (2003). The reminiscence circumplex and autobiographical memory functions. *Memory, 11,* 203–215.

Webster, J.D., Bohlmeijer, E.T., & Westerhof, G.J. (2010). Mapping the future of reminiscence: A conceptual guide for research and practice. *Research on Aging, 32*(4), 527–564.

Webster, J.D., & Haight, B.K. (1995). Memory lane milestones. In B. Haight & J.D. Webster (Eds.), *The art and science of reminiscing* (pp 37–48). Washington, DC: Taylor & Francis.

Weisberg, N., & Wilder, R. (2001). *Expressive arts with elders: A resource.* Philadelphia: Jessica Kingsley.

Weiser, J. (2002). Phototherapy techniques: Exploring the secrets of personal snapshots and family albums. *Journal of the Notre Dame Child & Family Institute,* Spring/Summer, 16–25.

Weismann, A. (1892). *Essays upon heredity and kindred biological problems.* Harvard University Archive: Claredon Press. Retrieved from http://books.google.com/books?id=hMcGAAAAYAAJ&oe=UTF-8

White, M. (2007). *Maps of narrative practice.* New York: W.W. Norton.

Williams, K. (2006). Improving outcomes of nursing home interactions. *Research in Nursing and Health, 29,* 121–133.

Williams, K.N., & Warren, C.A.B. (2009). Communication in assisted living. *Journal of Aging Studies, 23,* 24–36.

Yalom, I.D. (1995). *The theory and practice of group psychotherapy.* New York: Basic Books.

Yalom, I., & Leszcz, M. (2005). *The theory and practice of group psychotherapy* (5th ed.). New York: Basic Books.

Yalom, I.D., & Terrazas, F. (1968). Group therapy for psychotic elderly patients. *American Journal of Nursing, 68*(8), 1691–1694.

Zucchero, R.A. (1998). A unique model for training mental health professionals to work with older adults. *Educational Gerontology, 24*(3), 265–278.

RESOURCES

American Art Therapy Association, www.arttherapy.org Videos, articles, connections to art therapists.

Artress, Lauren, Rev. Dr. (2006). *Walking a sacred path*. Veridatas (Labyrinth), www.veriditas.org

Association for Gerontology in Higher Education, www.aghe.org

International Art Therapy Organization, www.internationalarttherapy.org

Leman, K. (2009). *The birth order book; Why you are the way you are*. Grand Rapids, MI: Revell.

National Association of Geriatric Education Centers, www.nagec.org

National Gerontological Nursing Association, www.ngna.org

National Remotivation Therapy Organization, Inc., (610) 767-5026, www.remotivation.com

Photo Therapy Centre, www.phototherapy-centre.com

Myers, J.E. (1992). *A treasury of senior humor.* Springfield, IL: Lincoln-Herndon Press.

The Harp Foundation, www.theharpfoundation.org

Therapeutic Thematic Arts Program (TTAT), Dr. Linda Vevine Madori, www.levinemadoriphd.com

INDEX